MANUAL
OF
SECTION

MANUAL OF SECTION

Lewis.Tsurumaki.Lewis

PAUL LEWIS, MARC TSURUMAKI, DAVID J. LEWIS

Princeton Architectural Press, New York

The Vertical Cut

INTRODUCTION

This book presents the means for understanding the complex and important role that section plays in architectural design and practice. Discussion and debate of a particular building's section are common in the study and practice of architecture. Yet there is no shared framework for the determination or evaluation of section. What are the different types of section, and what do they do? How does one produce those sections? Why would one choose to use one configuration of section over another? This book explores these questions and provides a conceptual, material, and instrumental framework for understanding section as a means to create architecture.

Our work has been motivated by the belief that the architectural section is key to architectural innovation. Given the environmental and material challenges that frame architectural practice in the twenty-first century, the section provides a rich and underexplored opportunity for inventively reimagining the intersection of structural, thermal, and functional forces. Moreover, the section is the site where space, form, and material intersect with human experience, establishing most clearly the relationship of the body to the building as well as the interplay between architecture and its context.

As practitioners and educators, we are invested equally in section as a type of representation and as a projective tool for spatial and material invention. We offer with this book a clear heuristic structure for a more robust discourse around the architectural section, to establish a shared basis for dialogue toward explorative and experimental architecture. Newly generated section perspectives of sixty-three significant built projects, organized into seven distinct types, provide students, architects, and other readers with a foundation for further cultivation of the section.

WHAT IS A SECTION?

We begin with the seemingly obvious question "What is a section?" In reference to architectural drawing, the term *section* typically describes a cut through the body of a building, perpendicular to the horizon line. A section drawing is one that shows a vertical cut transecting, typically along a primary axis, an object or building. The section reveals simultaneously its interior and exterior profiles, the interior space, and the material, membrane, or wall that separates interior from exterior, providing a view of the object that is not usually seen. This representational technique takes various forms and graphic conceits, each developed to illustrate different forms of architectural knowledge, from building sections that use solid fill or poche to emphasize the profile of the form, to construction details that depict materials through lines and graphic conventions. In an orthographic section the interior is also described through interior elevations of the primary architectural surfaces, while the combination of a section with a perspective describes in depth the interior as a space, using the techniques of perspectival projection.

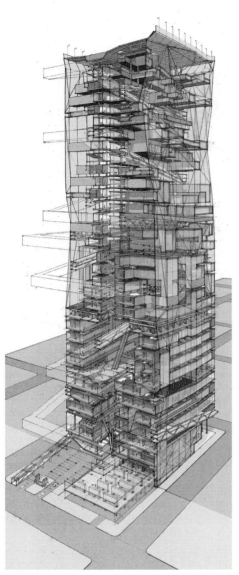

LTL Architects, Park Tower, 2004

Because the section begins with the visualization of that which will not be directly seen, it remains abstracted from the dominant way of understanding architecture through photographs and renderings. Sections provide a unique form of knowledge, one that by necessity shifts the emphasis from image to performance, from surface to the intersection of structure and materiality that comprises the tectonic logic of architecture. At the same time, section demonstrates the exchange among multiple aspects of embodied experience and architectural space, making explicit the intersection of scale and proportion, sight and view, touch and reach that is rendered visible in the vertical dimension (as opposed to from top down). In a section, the interior elevations of walls and surfaces are revealed, combining—for examination and exploration—structure and ornament, envelope and interior.

Plans and sections are similar representational conventions and offer an important point of comparison. Both depict a relationship that is not directly perceivable by the human eye, between a building's mass and the space. Both describe cuts—the one horizontal, the other vertical. The horizontal division of a plan cuts primarily through walls, not floors. Sections, on the other hand, are capable of showing cuts through both walls and floors and organize space in alignment with the size and scale of the standing human figure. Plans are typically argued to be the locus of design agency, with sections understood as a means to manifest the effects of the plan through structure and enclosure. In comparison to plan types, which are distinguished by their spatial consequences, section types are usually identified by the scale of their cut: site sections, building sections, wall sections, detail sections. Wall and detail sections foreground technical concerns, using graphic conventions of line, hatch, and tone, and depict material systems and tectonics. Site sections emphasize a built form's massing and its relationship with its environment and decrease the role of internal space. But it is in the building section that a number of crucial issues are at play, including the formal, social, organizational, political, spatial, structural, thermal, and technical.

CONTEMPORARY DISCOURSE ON SECTION

The section is not limited to its status as a representational technique. Today sections are used expansively to illustrate, test, and explore architectural designs. The section illuminates the interplay between a building's structure and the space framed between foundation and roof. Gravitational loads of structure trace vertically down through a building, with wind loads registering laterally against the side of a building's section. The material investment and spatial invention necessary to creatively resist these loads is best explored and depicted through the architectural section.

As questions of energy and ecology have become increasingly important to architectural design, the section will take on a more prominent role. Thermal forces work in section. Cold air is heavier and settles, while hot air rises. The sun rises and falls against the horizon. The vertical calibration of space is essential for inventing and creating architecture to engage environmental performance. Architects need to calibrate overhangs and apertures to produce

Revealing Cuts

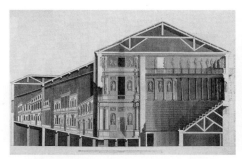

Ottavio Bertotti Scamozzi after Andrea Palladio, Teatro Olimpico, 1796

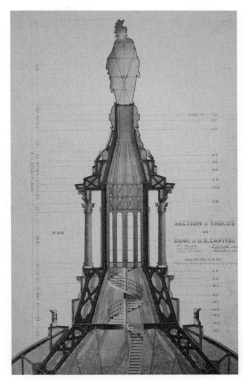

Thomas Ustick Walter, US Capitol Dome, 1859

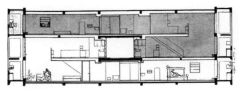

Le Corbusier, Unité d'Habitation, 1952

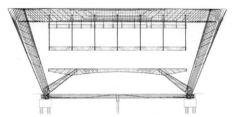

Affonso Eduardo Reidy, Museum for Modern Art, 1967

7

Thermal Sections

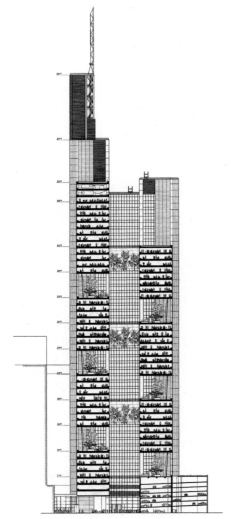

Candilis Josic Woods, Shading Diagram, 1968

Foster + Partners, Commerzbank Headquarters, 1997

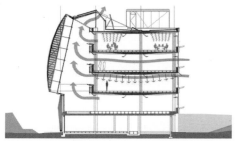

Bucholz McEvoy Architects, Limerick County Council, 2003

the optimal solar radiation; interiors should be configured to maximize convection-driven air movement; roof pitches need to be set to ensure the efficiency of solar panels; wall thickness must be dictated by insulation calculations; and so on. Often driven by a desire to meet sustainable certification criteria, architects and engineers use section drawings to illustrate adherence to conventions of thermal performance, with arrays of arrows illustrating thermodynamic forces. This emphasis on thermal efficiency foregrounds the opportunities of the section, but paradoxically constrains the spatial and experiential potential of the section by aligning sectional innovation to only functional obligations.

Yet, despite the importance of section as a drawing type and as a key method for optimizing spatial qualities, structural design, and thermal performance, there is a relative paucity of critical writings or discourse on section. A well-established body of writing exists on the history and impact of the plan, but there is no single book on the history, development, and use of the section within the practice of architecture. Only a few essays on section have been published, with the two most often cited written more than twenty-five years ago: Wolfgang Lotz's "The Rendering of the Interior in Architectural Drawings of the Renaissance"[1] and Jacques Guillerme and Hélène Vérin's "The Archaeology of Section."[2] Interestingly, both essays have parallel motives beyond cultivating and describing the architectural section itself.

This lack of direct attention may very well come from the ambiguous position that section occupies. It is often understood as a reductive drawing type, produced at the end of the design process to depict structural and material conditions in service of the construction contract, rather than as a means for the investigation of architectural form. While we are interested in the representational conditions of section, we argue that thinking and designing through section requires the building of a discourse about section, recognizing it as a site for invention.

HEURISTIC STRUCTURE FOR SECTIONS

The initial challenge in creating meaningful and accessible discussions of the section is the absence of a language that would provide a shared frame of reference. To address this void, we have devised a category system based on seven distinct section types: Extrusion, Stack, Shear, Shape, Hole, Incline, and Nest. The vast majority of sectional relationships can be described by one of these categories or several in combination. These types are intentionally reductive in order to make recognition simple; they are rarely found in pure form. Indeed, upon close inspection, no project perfectly demonstrates only one type of section, as all tend to have aspects of two or more. But where a dominant type of section prevails, that designation is given.

Our purpose is not to present these types as a new kind of Platonic ideal to be pursued in isolation. The fact that a building's section may exemplify one of these types does not automatically denote a particular significance or meaning. Rather, respectful of the potential of architecture, we provide these types as a heuristic frame for building a discourse about section at the intersection of material, cultural, and natural systems. Our objective is to learn more about the ways in which section types or combinations of types might be used and how this understanding could serve the discipline of architecture. As we argue, each type of section lends itself to distinct capacities, from the cultivation of a shared sense of space to the facilitation of thermal performance, from the establishment of spatial hierarchies to the enhancement of the interplay of exterior and interior.

The following terms and definitions will be explained in the subsequent essay in greater detail:

Extrusion: the direct extrusion of a plan to a height sufficient for the intended use

Stack: the layering of floors directly on top of one another—an extruded section, repeated with or without variations

Shape: the deformation of one or more of the primary horizontal surfaces of a building to sculpt space

Shear: the use of a rift or cut along either the horizontal or vertical axis of a building to generate sectional difference

Hole: the deployment of any number or scale of penetrations through a slab, exchanging lost floor area for benefits in section

Incline: the manipulation of the angle of an occupiable horizontal plane, which tilts the plan into section

Nest: the creation of sectional consequences through an interplay or overlap of legible volumes

Sixty-three one-point-perspective section drawings of built projects form the central portion of this book. We selected these projects because they represent a range of approaches to section, forming a body of work useful for further study, development, and inquiry. Certain projects illustrate one of the section types in a clear and demonstrative way. Other projects exhibit complex and creative approaches to section, often incorporating two or more types in a wide range of new formations that transcend the limits of a particular type in isolation.

All projects date from the turn of the twentieth century or later, a time frame chosen because of its historical alignment with the proliferation of standardized and industrialized methods of building. These methods typically have given rise to repetitive stacked sections, placing a new imperative on the section as a site of investigation and invention. We included only projects that have been built, to ensure that there would be sufficient documentary evidence to show the tectonic logic of the section and to verify that the complexity of the section did not come at the expense of constructability.

Although many existing publications analyze and assess these sixty-three projects, most do so by seeking to break each project into a series of discrete, easily digestible points. This reductive approach suggests that the comprehension of a building's complexity can be best achieved through categorizing concepts in isolation. Our approach is the opposite. We aim through a single, detailed drawing to demonstrate the range of intertwined issues that make architecture compelling. The section perspective intentionally

Section Perspectives

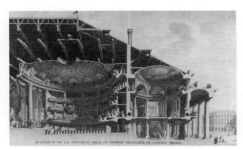

Charles de Wailly, Comédie-Française, 1770

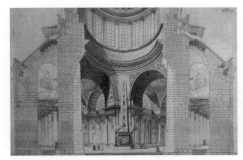

Jacques-Germain Soufflot, Pantheon, drawing by Alexandre-Théodore Brongniart, ca. 1796

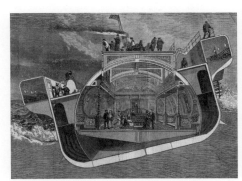

Henry Bessemer, saloon steamer, 1874

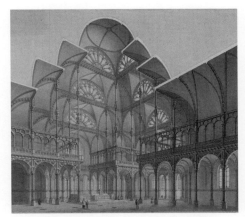

Louis-Auguste Boileau, system of interlocking arches, drawn by Tiburce-Sylvain Royol, ca. 1886

9

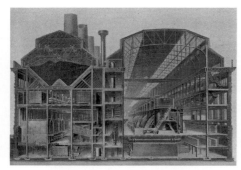

McKim, Mead & White, Interborough Rapid Transit Powerhouse, 1904

Jacques Hermant, Société Générale, 1912

Paul Rudolph, Yale Art and Architecture Building, 1963

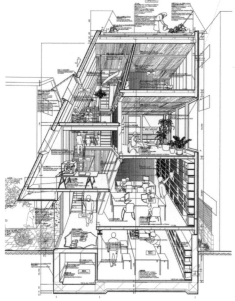

Atelier Bow-Wow, Bow-Wow House, 2005

combines the objective, measurable information of the section with the subjective visual logic of the perspective. As such, the drawings created for this book delineate facts and evidence while enticing the viewer into a rich spatial experience. The drawings are both abstract and immersive, analytical and illustrative. They build upon a history of this representational technique that includes such varied sources as the meticulous drawings of the École des Beaux-Arts; the analytical, technical drawings of the industrial era; Paul Rudolph's line rendering of complex spectacles; and Atelier Bow-Wow's hybrid mix of detailed construction drawings with outlines of interior activity.

Representing each project through a single section perspective with a standardized view allows comparison among and across projects. To create each drawing, we built a digital model and established a section cut true to the orientation of the page, not in oblique or perspective. We then set a single vanishing point, adjusting the perspective lens to bring interior or exterior surfaces into view, thus establishing a visual correspondence between the cut plane and the vertical surfaces that compose the projects. From each model, we exported a two-dimensional line drawing, which we adjusted and developed in a vector-based line program. The completed drawings follow the conventions of sectional drawings, where, for instance, the outside cut line that separates the edge of a solid surface and the open air or space beyond is marked by the thickest line, while lighter lines are used to illustrate secondary material distinctions within a cut solid or to describe the details of a surface viewed beyond the cutting plane.

These drawings differ from drawings of archaeological ruins, where the deterioration of a structure reveals its section to the observing eye. Since we cannot, of course, cut directly into built works, our representations depend on interpreting other drawings and images to create an accurate assessment of material conditions. These other drawings are themselves often approximations of construction yet to happen, thus raising compelling questions about historical accuracy and the construction of knowledge. The work of this book is based on photographs, drawings, descriptions, and, where possible, original archival construction drawings and/or digital files obtained directly from architects' firms. The drawings in this book are as precise as practicable, given available representations and the impossibility of absolute precision that is inherent to the section as a representational technique.

In addition to creating the sixty-three section perspectives, we have selected historically significant or otherwise compelling section drawings from throughout the history of architecture. These section images, which accompany the book's essays, include some unbuilt works in order to show the wide range of possibilities for using section to illustrate and generate architectural form. A chapter on the use of section as a generative tool for the work of our office, LTL Architects, complements the sixty-three projects. This work illustrates additional explorations in combining section and perspective, ones in which the section cut itself is put into perspective, as well as speculative projects, in which section is the generator for spatial and programmatic interplay.

Types and Performance of Section

Extrusion, Stack, Shear, Shape, Hole, Incline, and Nest are separate and primary methods for operating in section. For the sake of clarity, they are presented as distinct modes, but they rarely operate in isolation. Buildings exhibiting the most complex and intricate sections contain all manner of combinations. Nevertheless, the distinctions among the types provide a means to articulate how an architectural section is produced and to understand its effects.

EXTRUSION

The extrusion of a plan up to a height sufficient for the intended activity is the most basic form of section. An extruded section has little to no variation in the vertical axis. The vast majority of buildings are based on this efficiency, including most one-story office buildings, retail structures, big-box stores, factories, single-story houses, and apartments. Usually built with flat concrete slabs and rectilinear steel or wood frames, it produces the maximum usable square footage in relation to overall building volume. Elaboration of more complex sectional qualities is anathema to this model of efficiency. More complicated sections have the consequence of reducing valuable square footage of real estate. In extruded sections space is activated largely through plan and, to a lesser degree, elevation. It is a banal base against which other developments or types of section can be understood. This type of section usually lacks distinctive qualities, although in cases where an extrusion fails to meet typical models of efficiency, it can produce intriguing effects, including claustrophobia or agoraphobia. One can find examples of extrusions that are extremely low—for example, the half-floor sections found in Spike Jonze's film *Being John Malkovich*—or extremely high, such as the vast interior space of the Palace of Labor by Pier Luigi Nervi. In extruded sections, the ceiling is often the site of design investment, for reasons of structural articulation and the sheer extent of this surface.

Given that a straight extrusion is rarely remarkable, only a few of the buildings in this book are based solely on extrusion. A key condition of the extruded section is the role of the structure that separates the floor from the ceiling or roof. The Glass House by Philip Johnson places extraordinary emphasis on steel columns that rise from regular locations on the plan. The glass walls in effect turn the elevation into the section. The one anomaly of the system is the combined bathing area and fireplace, joined together to hide all the house's plumbing and heating systems behind the extruded figure of a brick cylinder, to preserve the clarity of the sectional diagram. While Johnson places the columns within the window wall external to the inhabitable space, Junya Ishigami does nearly the opposite with the Kanagawa Institute of Technology Workshop, dispersing or aggregating its columns to fill and frame the space as a field for different and adjustable uses. For Ishigami,

Extrusion Sections

Ralph Rapson and Eero Saarinen, Demountable Space, 1942

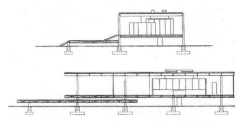

Ludwig Mies van der Rohe, Farnsworth House, 1951

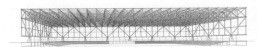

Ludwig Mies van der Rohe, Chicago Convention Center, 1954

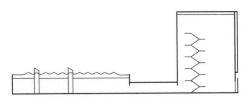

Arne Jacobsen, National Bank of Denmark, 1978

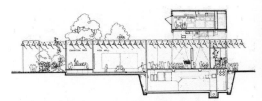

Renzo Piano, the Menil Collection museum, 1986

Stack Sections

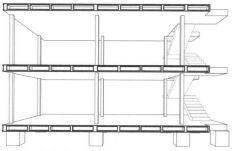

Le Corbusier, Maison Dom-ino, 1914

Antonin Raymond and Ladislav Rado, prototype for a department store, 1948

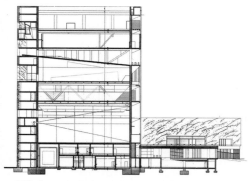

OMA, Center for Art and Media Technology, 1989

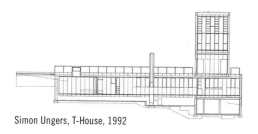

Simon Ungers, T-House, 1992

the extruded section heightens the distinction between the solid concrete base encasing and cantilevering the multiple thin columns and the highly articulated steel ceiling, whose pattern turns the structural diagram into ornament. While the two previous examples work within conventional extruded ceiling heights, in the Palace of Labor in Turin, Pier Luigi Nervi used the massive scale of mushroomlike columns to aggrandize an exhibition hall. Sixteen repetitive structural units define a 70-ft-high space. Although justified by pragmatics of construction speed and efficiency, the excessively tall space, animated by a grid of robust, tapered columns, transforms an extruded section into spectacle.

STACK

Stack is the placing of two or more floors or spaces on top of one another, with little connection among the individual stories. Stacking increases the real estate value of a property by expanding the square footage and usable capacity of a building without increasing its footprint. Financial gain is a basic motivation for the use of stacked section in architecture. Repetitive stacks are similar to extruded sections and can be deployed ad nauseam until limited by code, cost, or structural stability. Alternatively, stack can be created by placing very different floor types and shapes on top of one another. By itself, stacking does not produce interior effects. In office buildings or apartments, for example, each floor can be added with little or no consequence to the previous floors, beyond the impact on the quantity of vertical services required. It is precisely the ease of this accumulation that thwarts any sectional variations; its efficiency is based on the homogeneity of the section. It costs less to build the same floor than to introduce variations; all the expertise of Taylorism remains intact, from drawings to formwork to sequence of construction.

In buildings with single programs the extrusion rarely varies from floor to floor. Yet architects have exploited differences in the height of that extrusion on different stacked floors to allow for programmatic variation. A well-known example is Starrett & Van Vleck's Downtown Athletic Club, which comprises thirty-five levels with nineteen unique floor-to-floor heights, ranging from 6 ft (1.8 m) for a "bedroom utility" to a 23-ft-6-in (7.2 m) "gymnasium." Rem Koolhaas's influential analysis of the building in *Delirious New York* explicates the "culture of congestion" enacted within the building, where each of its "superimposed platforms" sponsors distinct uses, spaces, and experiences. The power of the building is derived from the sectional autonomy of each floor; the stacked section creates a form of seduction. "Each of the Club's floors is a separate installment of an infinitely unpredictable intrigue that extols the complete surrender to the definitive instability of life in the metropolis."[3] Critical to this reading is the fact that the Downtown Athletic Club's section cannot be experienced optically or synchronically. Rather, it is through the diachronic mechanism of the elevator that the narrative of programmatic and sectional disjunction unfolds. The Downtown Athletic Club is a peculiar project in that the fit between program and section is so precisely aligned, as gymnasiums, swimming pools, and handball and squash courts all require specific ceiling heights, and the relatively small footprint of the building allows each of these programs to inhabit its own floor.[4]

Whereas the Downtown Athletic Club conceals the variations of its section behind a muted facade, floor-to-floor variations in a stacked section have been used as the very image of other buildings: for example, MVRDV's Expo 2000 Netherlands Pavilion. Deploying the same logic used to create multilayered cakes, MVRDV juxtaposes completely different architectural spaces, from columnar halls filled with trees to a cast-concrete grotto, all topped by a trussed roof marked by wind turbines. Each floor is unique and varies substantially, demonstrating through the section an accumulation of different ways architecture engages environmental systems. Connection among the different stacked floors is made only through staircases and a bank of elevators clipped onto the exterior of the structure, reinforcing the independence of each zone.

Since stack is based on multiples, an alternate approach takes advantage of repetition, varying only floor heights to create difference. By adjusting the floor height while keeping the profile of each floor the same, SANAA created a distinctive building for the Dior flagship store, its seductiveness a product of the elegance of the architectural operation. In contrast, the individual galleries of Peter Zumthor's Kunsthaus Bregenz are treated as separate volumes, staggered and stacked with the same space between each floor. Services and lighting occupy the stacked spaces between the galleries, with the entire ensemble nested within a double-skin glass shell.

Ludwig Mies van der Rohe's work at S. R. Crown Hall at IIT disguises the stacked section behind a singular architectural form. In truth, the monumental exposed structural beams that mark the profile of the building only support the ceiling of the main floor. A more utilitarian lower floor sits below, half-sunken into the ground and supported by load-bearing walls. The exterior curtain wall, marked by continuous vertical steel members, cloaks the section's stacking, reinforcing the impression of a singular spatial volume.

The stacked section limits the thermodynamic movement of air and water. In order for these systems to serve a building, they must be pumped, pushed, and ducted vertically beyond a single floor. Louis I. Kahn's design for the Salk Institute exploits this isolating condition to full effect. To accommodate the extensive mechanical services needed for research labs and ensure that those spaces would be column-free, Kahn layered on top of each laboratory a full floor dedicated to systems threaded through an open Vierendeel truss system. Three successive pairings of lab and service zone make up the stacked section.

SHAPE

Shaping is the sculpting of space through the deformation of a continuous horizontal surface or surfaces. This adds a particular volume or form to the section and can occur in a floor or a ceiling or both. Shapes can exhibit an extremely wide range of topologies.[5] The ceiling is a more common location for this modulation

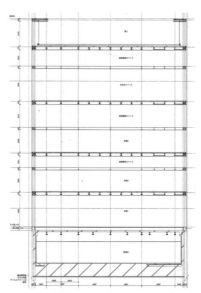

SANAA, Christian Dior Omotesando, 2003

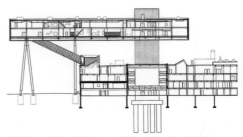

Will Alsop, Ontario College of Art and Design, 2004

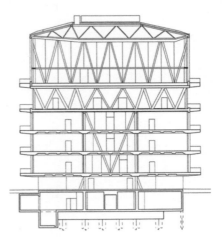

Christian Kerez, school in Leutschenbach, 2009

GLUCK+, Tower House, 2012

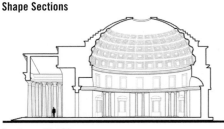

Pantheon, AD 128

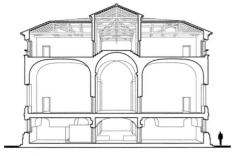

Andrea Palladio, Villa Foscari, 1560

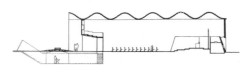

Eladio Dieste, Church of Christ the Worker, 1952

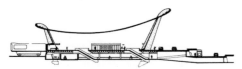

Eero Saarinen, Dulles Airport, 1962

Hans Scharoun, Berlin Philharmonic Concert Hall, 1963

Kenzo Tange, Yoyogi National Gymnasium, 1964

than the floor, as variations in a ceiling do not affect a plan's efficacy. Load-bearing masonry cathedrals, covered stadiums, igloos, and tents all have shaped sections. Buildings with shaped sections frequently exhibit a close fit between their structure and their section, often incorporating vaults, shells, domes, and tensile membranes, with the shaping of the roof aligning with gravitational load paths and structural spans. Much of the work of Félix Candela demonstrates quite clearly the intersection of structural forces and shape in section, as in his design for Los Manantiales Restaurant, consisting of a thin-shell concrete roof cast into hyperbolic-paraboloid forms. The project is in essence a physical manifestation of a structural diagram. Marcel Breuer's Hunter College Library is another example of a structural form, in this case assembling a flowering column module into a repetitive shaped section. Using more conventional framing, Rudolph M. Schindler's Bennati Cabin is constructed from two-by studs organized into triangles, forming an early example of an A-frame house. The shape is structurally efficient, permitting a large living floor below a narrower sleeping loft, with the triangular shape fulfilling local ordinance's request for alpine exterior aesthetics.

The dominance of flat-slab construction in the past century has decreased the frequency of this type of section, as the separation of structure from enclosure, exemplified by Le Corbusier's Maison Dom-ino housing prototype, shifted the articulation of space from section to plan. As Colin Rowe wryly notes about Le Corbusier's Villa Stein in "The Mathematics of the Ideal Villa," "Free plan is exchanged for free section."[6] Shaped section can be found in buildings where an intensification of social space and gathering is needed, including most buildings of collective worship. In churches and synagogues the ceiling can be used to establish a focal point within a unified volume.

The Pantheon and Le Corbusier's Notre Dame du Haut are both sacred buildings with a shaped section, one concave, the other convex. Both use the section to calibrate the play of natural light in the space, and in both the section of the ceiling is aligned with the structure to varying degrees. In a more secular context, Alvar Aalto deployed a complex, sculpted ceiling to reinforce the legibility of different areas within the single open space of his library in Seinäjoki, Finland, as well as to control daylight in the stacks. In addition, Aalto stepped the floor, setting a reading room a half-story down in the middle of the space to provide a sense of privacy while still preserving visibility from the circulation desk above.

A modulated ceiling is frequently limited to a single-story building or to a building's top floor, as the ceiling's other side can be hard to occupy without the introduction of poche, dropped ceilings, or soffits. As such, a desire to manipulate a structure's exterior to protect the interior space from the forces of nature can be a catalyst for using this section type and often informs the shape of the roof. This use of shape is clearly in evidence in Jørn Utzon's double-layered roof system for the Bagsværd Church, where a complex, curvilinear interior ceiling is covered by a simplified rectilinear shed. The section reveals the potential for a loose fit between an exterior shape responding to the obligation of weather enclosure and an interior ceiling that modulates light, sound, and space for sacred purposes. Steven Holl's project Cité de l'Océan et du Surf presents a very different reason for a shaped roof. Here the top of the building is an occupiable outdoor surface, shaped to reflect the waves associated with surfing.

When a shaped section occurs in the floor, causing a disruption to the horizontal plan, it can cluster or choreograph collective programs, particularly those based on stasis. Theaters, auditoriums, and churches frequently use a shaped section in the floor. It is also common for these building types to have adjustments to their ceiling, often for acoustic reasons. While usually described exclusively with regard to its sloped floor, Claude Parent and Paul Virilio's Church of Sainte-Bernadette du Banlay equally displays section deformed by shape, with the roof and floor sculpted and aligned to reinforce the spatial reading of the volume set on an incline. Similarly, the design of SANAA's Rolex Learning Center aligns the shaping of the floor slab and the ceiling slab, but not within a rectilinear envelope. Instead, the space between the underside and the ground is visible and activated. As a hybrid project, the center can be characterized as an unusual combination of an extruded section and a shaped section activated by holes. Similarly, Toyo Ito's Taichung Metropolitan Opera House uses shape in combination with other types of section. However, it is the sculpted concrete forms that dominate, set in contrast to the repetitively stacked floor plates and active in the section, providing the key spaces throughout the project.

It's instructive to note, however, the distinction between the sectional transformations of shaped floors and those of complex topography. In large-scale projects such as the Yokohama Ferry Terminal by Foreign Office Architects or the Olympic Sculpture Park by Weiss/Manfredi, the sectional profile tends toward landscape, with the topography of the landform not oriented necessarily toward the creation of interior architectural space. As these projects expand in size and/or merge into the topographic conditions of the site, their sections are experienced and understood less as shaped surfaces and more as extensions or transformations of landscapes.

SHEAR

Shear involves a rift or cut parallel to either the horizontal or vertical axis of section. The subdesignations of vertical and horizontal shear are necessary, since each creates completely different sectional operations and effects.

Vertical shear, where floor plates are cut and levels adjusted vertically, means that discontinuity in plan is coupled with new forms of continuity in section. Vertical shear is particularly effective at inducing optical, thermal, or acoustic connections within an extruded or stacked section without significantly compromising the tectonic efficiencies of repetition. This intriguing friction can be used for different purposes. Split-level suburban houses provide greater visual connection and flow between floors than two-story houses. Typically, an entry combined with a kitchen and

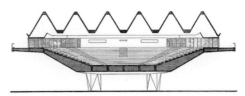

Johannes Hendrik van den Broek, Delft Auditorium, 1966

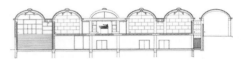

Louis I. Kahn, Kimbell Art Museum, 1972

OMA, Agadir Convention Center, 1990

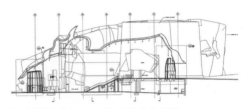

Frank Gehry, Experience Music Project, 2000

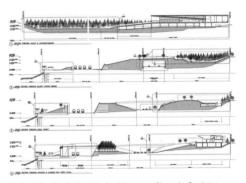

Weiss/Manfredi, Seattle Art Museum: Olympic Sculpture Park, 2007

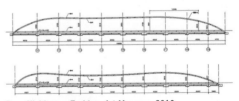

Ryue Nishizawa, Teshima Art Museum, 2010

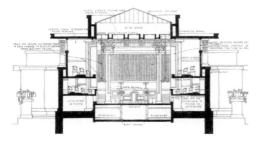

Frank Lloyd Wright, Unity Temple, 1906

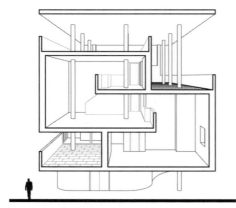

Le Corbusier, Villa Baizeau, 1928

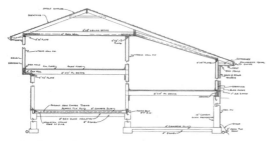

A. J. Rynkus, Split-Level House, 1958

Paul Rudolph, Beekman Penthouse Apartment, 1973

dining area is located halfway between a lower-level garage and a more formal living room, with bedrooms above the entry. Rather than simply serving as a connection between discrete floors, the staircase in the split-level house can be argued to be synthetic with the various floors, making the house an extension of the logic of the stair.

In Herman Hertzberger's design for the Apollo Schools, a vertical shear allows for enhanced visual exchange among classrooms and hallways, encouraging theatrical social dynamics while simultaneously allowing the majority of the classroom spaces to be tucked beyond diagonal sight lines. This creates what Hertzberger calls "the right balance between view and seclusion."[7] More extreme juxtapositions between plan and section can be intensified through a vertical shear. Diller Scofidio + Renfro uses vertical shear in Brown University's Granoff Center for the Creative Arts to induce visual dialogue between otherwise disconnected programs, with very little of each program hidden or secluded. This intensification of optical disjunction across programs is registered by a glass wall at the shear line that serves to mitigate sound transmission. Vertical shear can generate intricate relationships between the inside and the outside of a building at the top or bottom of a shear rather than just around the perimeter, because the staggering of levels can carry through the building from the bottom to the top. Vertical shear requires limited change to the footprint or boundary of the exterior walls and is often used to create internal spatial difference for buildings on tight sites.

A horizontal shear maintains continuity in plan and some of the logic of extruded floor plates, but produces spaces through the interplay between setback and cantilever. While a vertical shear directly impacts the interior, a horizontal shear largely affects the exterior. Two other factors affect buildings with horizontal shear. One is the degree to which the shear is applied systematically and regularly to each floor. The other, which is usually directly related to the first, is the degree of similarity among the different floor plates. Henri Sauvage's designs for stepped houses, best exemplified by his apartment building at 13 Rue des Amiraux in Paris, exhibit both a consistently repeated horizontal shear and relatively equal floor plates, producing a series of terraces on the setback side of the shear. In this raked diagram, one side of the building is opened up to the sun and sky, while the other defines a space, cast in shadow, between the cantilevers and the ground. Sauvage placed two raked buildings back to back and filled the underbelly with a swimming pool, effectively creating both private benefits (terraces) and collective benefits (pool) through this one sectional operation. This diagram was highly seductive, particularly for housing, as it injected into the model of the stacked slab tower in the park both superior solar exposure/views and a space rife with collective potential. It efficiently deployed repetition to produce difference. Moreover, it made legible new part-to-whole relationships and allowed for greater continuities between the landscape and the building. Horizontal shear was instrumental in a number of projects and buildings, including Walter Gropius's Wohnberg (1928 proposal), Le Corbusier's Durand Project (1933, Algiers),

Paul Rudolph's Lower Manhattan Expressway (1972 proposal), Denys Lasdun's residence halls for University of East Anglia (1962, Norwich, UK) and Christ's College (1966, Cambridge, UK), Ricardo Legorreta's Hotel Camino Real (1981, Mexico City), and more recently BIG/JDS's the Mountain Dwellings. The Mountain brings to fruition one of Sauvage's century-old diagrams, which situates parking beneath a pyramid of sheared housing. The fact that the Mountain contains more parking than needed for the apartments demonstrates that as the amount of the rake or the angle is increased, thereby producing more exterior space for each apartment, an engorged underside can result.

Horizontal shear can create collective social spaces when a sequence of terraces are combined into a single open volume. The Barnard College Diana Center by Weiss/Manfredi cleverly deploys horizontal shear internal to the building mass to open up a series of public lounges stitched together within a multistory academic building, creating visual continuity on the diagonal through the urban campus. Similarly, Neutelings Riedijk's Netherlands Institute for Sound and Vision takes full advantage of the spatial continuity created by horizontal shear, with the orientation of the shear operating at ninety-degree angles below and above grade. The entry lobby is connected visually to a series of stepped levels of the building's subterranean archive. The stacked floors above are sheared in the perpendicular direction, opening up the main space to daylight from the skylight, simultaneously creating a multilevel exhibition volume at the top. The cumulative effect is a ziggurat-shaped void carved from the building mass.

Repetitive horizontal shear on self-similar floor plates produces a combination of staggered exterior spaces, deploying corbeling for stability. The use of horizontal shear in varying amounts creates sectional moments around the full perimeter of a building, often relying on a central core for balance. These moments are more local than a repetitive raked section and can take the form of an accumulation of platforms, balconies, overhangs, and skylights, rather than collective spaces. Frank Lloyd Wright's Fallingwater is a good example of different-size floor slabs that are dispersed to activate sectional effects on the exterior of a building. They twist around the whole of the exterior of the building, producing simultaneous sensations of upward growth and downward cascade, while the interior is compressed, with space pushed horizontally, not vertically.

HOLE

A pragmatic and frequently used sectional device, the hole is a cut or penetration through a slab that exchanges lost floor area for benefits in section. Holes are spatial commodities that can be tactically deployed for vertical effects. They range in scale and quantity from a single small opening between two floors to multiple large atria that organize whole buildings.

Small holes accommodate infrastructural runs, such as risers, ducts, and chase spaces; they are typically not large enough to impact the structural integrity of the floor. The shafts of elevators and fire stairs are used to strengthen an overall structure, with

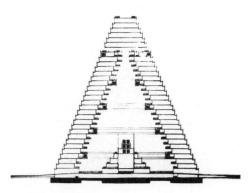

Walter Gropius, Wohnberg proposal, 1928

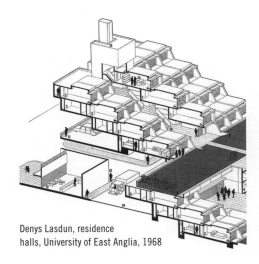

Denys Lasdun, residence halls, University of East Anglia, 1968

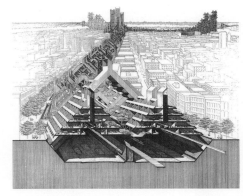

Paul Rudolph, Lower Manhattan Expressway proposal, 1972

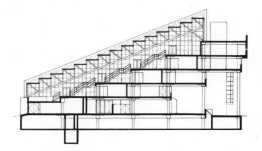

John Andrews, Gund Hall, Harvard Graduate School of Design, 1972

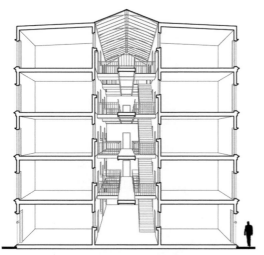

Marie-Gabriel Veugny, la Cité Napoléon, 1853

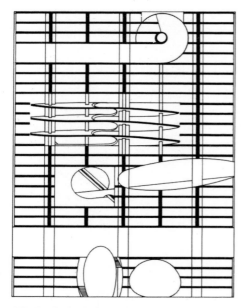

OMA, Très Grande Bibliothèque, 1989

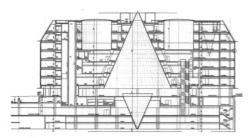

Jean Nouvel and Emmanuel Cattani & Associates, Galeries Lafayette, 1996

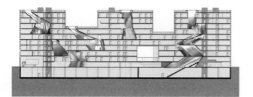

Steven Holl Architects, Simmons Hall, MIT, 2002

solid walls often acting to resist lateral shear forces; they are inserted within vertical holes precisely because these spaces are not expected to produce visual continuity between floors.[8] Small holes through single floor plates can be strategically located based on plan imperatives.

Large holes are more substantial voids in a multistory building, creating spatial continuity among floors. These holes are predicated on some form of visual exchange and allow for light, acoustic, olfactory, and thermal continuity within a building. Holes are a second order of sectional operation, acting on a given single or multilevel stacked section.

A clear and basic manifestation of a hole at the scale of a room is found in Le Corbusier's Maison Citrohan, realized at the 1927 Weissenhofsiedlung exhibition in Stuttgart, Germany. Its central organizing spatial component is the double-height void made by cutting back a substantial portion of the second floor. In addition to allowing exchanges of light, view, and sound, this hole establishes hierarchies between public and private, figure and ground, and part and whole. There is a clarity and simplicity to this two-story section. It does not require a new construction system; it just edits back the given structure. This scale of hole influences the importance and hierarchy of spaces around it, creating, for instance, formal double-height spaces. Lobbies, central meeting areas, interior courtyards, and domestic living rooms all make use of this type of program-specific scaled hole.[9]

Atria amplify the scale of smaller holes, in terms of both width and quantity of floors, and exceed their effect. This increased scale permits the effective distribution of daylight (often from skylights) and movement of air, and heightens the role of the interior. Wright's Larkin Building used the central atrium to organize and focus the program of its offices, allowing sunlight in and assisting with the mechanical distribution of air. Moreover, in this large and sealed building, wisely separated from the din and soot of the neighboring rail yard outside, the atrium replaced the exterior as the building's focus.

At this scale, the atrium is less a cut through floors than a space around which floors are built, a condition Louis I. Kahn made explicit in the articulated structural lining of the atrium of the library at Phillips Exeter Academy. In the asymmetrical Ford Foundation Headquarters by Kevin Roche John Dinkeloo and Associates, the atrium serves as a conditioned, four-season garden, open to sunlight on the south and east sides. Offices on the north and west envelop the atrium, with selective use of horizontal shear to terrace the ground and rooftop enclosure.

John Portman has pushed the use of the atrium to an extreme, creating hotels that are defined by the radical dichotomy between their conventional exteriors and spectacular interiors. The vast atria of his interiors appear to extend upward infinitely, a sensation heightened by exposed glass elevators accelerating past series of stacked open walkways and balconies. The atrium of Portman's New York Marriott Marquis hotel is framed by thirty-seven stories of rooms, stacked in groups of five floors that illustrate local horizontal shear. The visual pleasure and spectacle of atria account for their frequent use in places of consumption, notably department stores, as exemplified by Galeries Lafayette in Paris of 1912 and Jean Nouvel's design for the same company in Berlin at the end of the twentieth century.

Holes are the key component of Toyo Ito's Sendai Mediatheque, striking an intriguing balance between their implications for the plan and the legibility of the section. The building is organized around thirteen holes, which puncture all seven floor slabs. The holes serve as the locus of circulation; as mechanical shafts; as tubes for the flow of energy, air, light, and sound through the floors; and, paradoxically, as the building's structure. These hollow, inhabitable tubes made through bundled steel columns not only produce the section but become primary plan components, choreographing the program on each floor. In the Sendai Mediatheque, holes ringed by structure animate what would otherwise be a series of repetitive and independent stacked floors.

INCLINE

Inclines are sloped floor surfaces, which often connect levels. Inclines change the angle of an occupiable horizontal plane, thus effectively rotating plan into section. Unlike stacks, shears, and holes, inclines blur the distinction between plan and section. With inclines, sectional play does not require the sacrifice of a portion of the plan. Like holes, their specific impact on section is dependent on their scale; they can range from a narrow ramp to a full floor to entire built environments, as envisioned by Claude Parent and Paul Virilio in their oblique urban order. Le Corbusier proposed the *promenade architecturale*, an itinerary through space based on the continuity of the horizontal with ramps. In its first realization in 1923, with Villa La Roche–Jeanneret, a single ramp cuts one level through a gallery. At this scale, the incline is more of an object within a double-height space than a fully formed component of the building's section. This ramp has a stronger impact in plan, where its curve highlights a bulge in the wall. In comparison, the incline in Villa Savoye is much more instrumental in organizing and activating the entire building as a *promenade architecturale*. It connects space in, up, through, and out of the two floor slabs, culminating in a roof garden atop the building. However, the vertical space of section is truncated by the fact that the ramp fills the area that was removed from the floors in order to accommodate it. Moreover, the ramp moves from inside to outside and is spatially disconnected inside the villa, where Le Corbusier relied on the continuity of the wall adjacent to the ramp to register the section. This reading is substantiated by the section drawing for Villa Savoye included in his *Oeuvre complète*, which is from an earlier scheme, in which that wall extended up another floor. Somewhat ironically, a narrow ramp such as the one in Villa Savoye produces more discontinuity than continuity in plan. Even though the ramp is only four feet wide, it requires thirty-two feet to make the connection between the two floors.[10] The incline viewed in the path of travel along the ramp creates continuity of section, but this comes at a price. In order to connect different floors, the incline must also cut into the plan of the villa,

Incline Sections

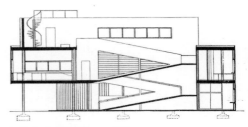

Le Corbusier, Villa Savoye, 1931

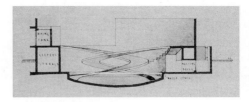

Tecton, Penguin Pool, 1934

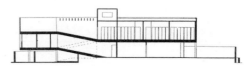

Vilanova Artigas, Almeida House, 1949

Le Corbusier, Palais des Congrès, 1964

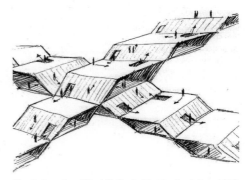

Claude Parent and Paul Virilio, habitable circulation, 1966

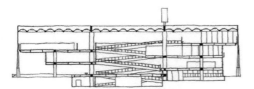

Vilanova Artigas, São Paulo School of Architecture, 1969

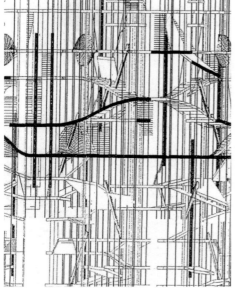

OMA, Jussieu-Two Libraries (detail), 1992

OMA, Educatorium, 1997

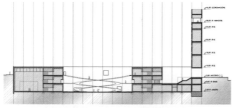

Alberto Campo Baeza, Museum of Memory, 2009

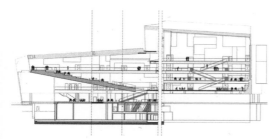

Henning Larsen Architects, Harpa, 2011

creating a discontinuity of space. The ramp at the Villa Savoye cuts the plan in two, distinguishing the garage from the entry hall and the exterior terrace from interior bedrooms, while enabling light and views to pass diagonally across the ramp.

This paradox of an incline creating continuity in section only through discontinuity in plan was examined and explored by Frank Lloyd Wright in two different projects. In the V. C. Morris Gift Shop, a narrow ramp is aligned with an atrium, thereby enhancing visual connections across the section and decreasing the disruptions to the space from shear. Movement up and, more important, around this incline adds to the spectacle of shopping. While the incline in Villa Savoye is autonomous, as it splits the column grid and penetrates through all floors, the incline in the Morris Gift Shop appears to be hung from the balustrade of the floor above, allowing the circulation on the ground floor to slide in and around it. Because the Morris Gift Shop was an insertion into an existing building, Wright's play with the incline was constrained, but he explored this theme further in the Solomon R. Guggenheim Museum. In this well-known museum as spiral, Wright fuses an incline and atrium, turning the main gallery floors into a single continuous promenade. (Side galleries and support spaces have flat floors and are located away from the central event.) Since all floors merge into a single surface, the challenge for the viewer is not an issue of sequence or passage but rather starting point. Wright famously insisted that all visitors first entertain an elevator ride to the top, with the downward slope of the incline facilitating a leisurely walk. (Curators have not always followed Wright's commands when designing show sequences.)

Wright's work on the Guggenheim draws parallels to his unbuilt Gordon Strong Automobile Objective and Planetarium project, where a double-helix ramp brings cars up and down. Designs for roads and parking systems have deployed incline as a necessary means of facilitating automobile passage. Ramped parking structures use inclines in two distinct manners: either as connecting pieces among level floors of repetitively stacked parking or as continuously ramped surfaces that merge parking and circulation. The Guggenheim plays on the latter, while Herzog & de Meuron's 1111 Lincoln Road explores the creative possibilities of the former, introducing variations in floor height to transform a parking structure into a social destination, complete with a residence with sheared floor plates on top.

While Wright negotiates the paradox of the ramp creating discontinuity by introducing the central atrium in the Guggenheim, OMA deploys the incline to foster greater programmatic density and to create visual juxtapositions. OMA's Rotterdam Kunsthal is a cut-back incline at the scale of a whole building. The shear between two inclined surfaces is exaggerated and animates programmatic misalignments, with a single incline that is split by a wall of glass into an interior corridor moving up and an exterior path that threads through the center of the building. The outer edges of this incline are pushed to the exterior and are legible as elevations. OMA's unbuilt project for Jussieu (1992) is organized around a continuous incline, which, like the

Guggenheim, eradicates floor-to-floor distinctions. But unlike at the Guggenheim, the width of the incline expands and contracts and, more important, tactically deploys discontinuity within that surface through cuts, folds, and shears, to allow for a multiplicity of programs and spaces on the same continuous surface.

Although one objective of a continuous inclined surface is an activation of the section, the consequence is not necessarily an intriguing vertical space. This is because an inclined surface often folds back on itself, effectively forming a stacked section with unlevel floors. In these projects, vertical extensions of space are produced by editing back or removing parts of the floor, as in the Guggenheim's atrium or the vertical shafts in the Kunsthal or Jussieu.[11] Continuous inclined surfaces often exhibit shear and need holes for visual continuity. This is clearly evident in Henning Larsen's Moesgaard Museum, where the shape of the building is defined by its inclined, sloped green roof. Whereas the incline is obvious on the exterior, it is primarily visually apparent within the interior when viewed through a large hole for the building's oversized staircase.

NEST

Nests produce sections through interplay or overlap between discrete volumes. Whereas stack, shear, hole, and incline work primarily with flat plates, a nest positions three-dimensional figures or volumes for sectional effect. The early twentieth-century houses of Adolf Loos often demonstrate volumetric nesting, with rooms stacked on various levels to create complex spatial sequences, typically described as *Raumplan*. The spatial, structural, or environmental performance of the nest usually exceeds that of the volumes operating in isolation. Crucial in this approach to section is the functionality of interstitial space and its relationship to the exterior skin. Although the permutations of a nested section are numerous, a handful of examples will help explicate two significant variations.

To create the Center for Arts in La Coruña, Spain, aceboXalonso Studio lodged a series of highly specific performance spaces as distinct but interconnected forms within a box formed by a multilayered skin. The resulting interior is a complicated vertical space that moves around the volumes. The volumes are programmatically specific, whereas the space of the section between is indeterminate, fluid, and undefined. As the performance spaces press up against the exterior, the double skin of the shell is interrupted, thus making visible on the outside the nesting of the volumes in section. MVRDV's Effenaar Cultural Center is based on a more pragmatic approach. Individual rooms, each with its own size and function, are arrayed around the exterior of the building's skin, in effect increasing the thickness of that skin. These generate a doughnut in section, with a main concert hall as the center of the doughnut, thereby linked to all the individual programs in the building. Whereas aceboXalonso begins with a large frame into which smaller programs are nested, MVRDV organizes the nested volumes to create the overall figure, building the whole from individual parts.

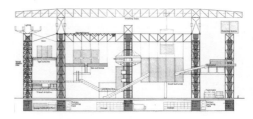

Cedric Price, Fun Palace, 1964

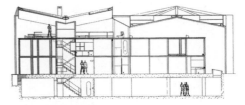

Le Corbusier, Heidi Weber Museum, 1967

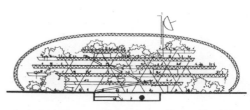

Buckminster Fuller and Norman Foster, Climatroffice, 1971

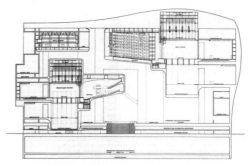

Jean Nouvel and Philippe Starck, Tokyo Opera House, 1986

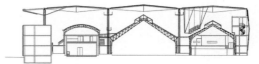

Bernard Tschumi, Le Fresnoy Art Center, 1992

FAR frohn&rojas, Wall House, 2007

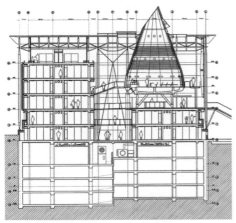

Richard Rogers, Bordeaux Law Courts, 1998

MVRDV, Eyebeam Museum of Art and Technology, 2001

Vertical circulation in these and other nested projects is a key design challenge, as stairs run the risk of disrupting the tight set of adjacent volumes. In Loos's designs, stairs are woven in and among nested volumes, becoming at times part of a sequence of the vertical staggering of volumes and at other moments hidden and tucked away, existing in the space between rooms. With the Effenaar Cultural Center, MVRDV simply moved the circulation and fire staircases to the exterior, where they exist as independent spaces attached from outside.

MVRDV's 2001 proposal for the Eyebeam Institute is a more nuanced and intricate approach to nesting. As with Effenaar, individual program pieces are dispersed in section, but here they are separated from one another. The consequence is a complex interstitial void punctuated by the shapes of those program pieces. Moreover, the exterior skin, which doubles as structure, extends around these pieces into the building volume, effectively bridging between pieces and stiffening the exterior structure. Apertures on the exterior of the building replace the structural skin where the interior volumes kiss that skin. The specificity of these nested interiors' programs is visible on the exterior, yet this specificity is occluded from view within the larger building cavity. As with the two previous projects, the interstitial space is programmatically indeterminate, permitting unforeseen activities to be catalyzed by the spatial stimulation of an open and compelling section.

These previous three examples all deploy discrete volumes adjacent to one another to activate an interstitial section. A different category of nesting occurs when discrete volumes are lodged inside one another. Although the logic of this type of nesting would seem to undermine the development of section, this redundancy, when intelligently deployed, can intensify the programmatic relationship between the volumes. It can also produce new models of thermal performance based on a complex relationship between exterior and interior conditioned spaces. A small-scale example of this type is Charles Moore's own house in Orinda, California, from 1962, where the volumes of the sitting area and the shower, each marked by four columns and a skylight, are caught within the overall shell of the small house. These "aedicules" invert both the normal structure of the house and the conventional location of the bath, which here is open to the whole house. These nested volumes become the primary structure of the house, allowing its exterior corners to disappear as sliding doors. Counterintuitively, this nesting sponsors greater openness and connection between the exterior and the most private interior. A different manipulation of the expected logic of nesting is found in the San Paolo Parish Complex in Foligno, Italy, by Fuksas Architects. Large, hollow sleeves structurally connect the two volumes, suspending the inner volume and channeling sunlight into this innermost space, bypassing the outer volume. The contrast in both the volume and illumination of the section add dramatic effect to the church. Nesting is a particularly good sectional device for manipulating and controlling daylight through multiple layered skins, a technique used by Gordon Bunshaft of Skidmore, Owings & Merrill at the Beinecke Library. Here a box of translucent stone protects rare books from the damaging effects of direct sun, while placing them on dramatic display within their own internalized glass vitrine, nested inside the exterior envelope.

An extremely literal example of a nested section is Sou Fujimoto's House N. The three rectangular layers of this house are all white, contain self-similar rectangular framed openings on all five sides, and diminish only slightly in thickness from outer- to innermost. Yet, by locating the thermal enclosure on the middle layer and by pushing the outer skin to the limits of property, Fujimoto conscripts the grounds as the site of a surprisingly complex homogeneity that blurs conventional distinctions between interior and exterior, private and public. Although all the layers look alike, each does different things: the outer defines the pre- cinct of the house; the middle regulates the thermal environment; and the inner distinguishes bedrooms from the living/dining area. Each alone would be too porous, but collectively they regulate privacy and view. Nonetheless, the layers do little to increase the environmental performance of the house, as it is only the middle layer that acts as the thermal barrier. In contrast, the Mont-Cenis Training Center by Jourda Architectes uses sequential nesting to enhance thermal performance. Two unremarkable linear buildings are located under a very large wood shed, which spans beyond the footprints of the inner buildings. Clad in glass and photovoltaic panels, the outer skin uses passive solar and ventilation to modify extremes in weather, producing a temperate thermal layer between the outside and the two inhabited buildings. Neither fully inside nor fully outside, this space is conceptually and functionally akin to the cavity between two panes of glass in a thermal window. Furthermore, nesting makes possible a gradient of thermal con- ditions directly linked to the complex interplay of space, building materials, and thermodynamic forces in section. Mont-Cenis Training Center is a more refined elaboration of the exterior ther- mal or climate utopias envisioned by Buckminster Fuller. Whether in his conceptual dome to encapsulate Manhattan or the United States Pavilion at Expo '67 in Montreal, Fuller repeatedly used nested section to generate controlled thermal environments. These large-scale nested sections were the product of his exploration and innovations in space-frame construction systems, which allow for the building of expansive envelopes, facilitating the placement of buildings within buildings.

HYBRIDS

Extrusion, Stack, Shape, Shear, Hole, Incline, and Nest are primary methods for operating in section. For the sake of clarity, they have been presented as distinct modes, but they rarely oper- ate in isolation. Hole and Shear, for instance, require the exis- tence of extruded floors or stacked sections to register the action. Shaped sections typically couple with stacked plates to provide sufficient support and service spaces. Indeed, buildings exhibiting the most complex and intricate sections contain all manners of combinations. We have included projects that exemplify innovative combinations of section types, often in creative tension; where no single dominant type is in evidence, we have designated these projects Hybrids.

Hybrid Sections

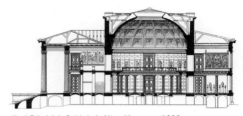

Karl Friedrich Schinkel, Altes Museum, 1830

Charles Garnier, Paris Opéra, 1875

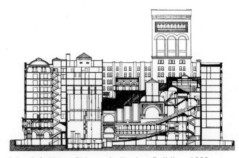

Adler & Sullivan, Chicago Auditorium Building, 1889

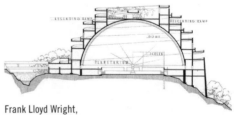

Frank Lloyd Wright,
Gordon Strong Automobile Objective, 1925

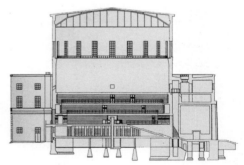

Erik Gunnar Asplund, Stockholm Public Library, 1928

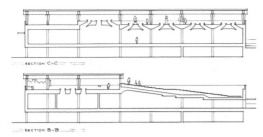

Alvar Aalto, Art Museum in Baghdad, 1958

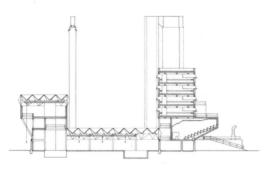

James Stirling, James Gowan, and Michael Wilford,
Leicester University Engineering Building, 1963

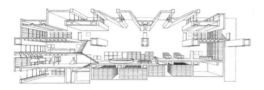

Arata Isozaki, Oita Prefectural Library, 1966

John Portman, Hyatt Regency San Francisco, 1974

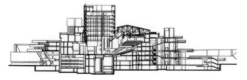

Denys Lasdun, Royal Theater, 1976

Hybrids exhibit instructive strategies for combining sections. A basic strategy is the juxtaposition of two very different section types where neither is dominant. Michael Maltzan's design for the Star Apartments, for instance, joins stacking and nesting. The concrete podium with residential floors above establishes stack as a key sectional approach. Yet the modular construction of the individual apartment units dictates a nested approach within the upper stacked system.

Other hybrid projects synthesize sectional strategies so seamlessly that understanding their intersection of systems requires close examination. The Villa Girasole—with its lightweight rotating top that is set on a rusticated base and connected through an eight-story spiral stair tower—demonstrates nested forms on top of one another, stacked floors that compose the house and occupiable base, and a sizable hole in the figure of the spiral staircase. The overall building is sheared horizontally by the landscape, with the atrium stair tower providing continuity between upper and lower gardens. In Herzog & de Meuron's VitraHaus, shaped volumes are nested into each other, stacked together, and then sheared horizontally to produce an exterior atrium. Arguably the most synthetic project, demonstrating multiple merged section types, is SANAA's Rolex Learning Center, where a simple extrusion is continuously shaped, creating inclined surfaces and intersecting with a series of discrete holes to reveal the project's deformed section.

Not surprisingly, multistory buildings that are organized vertically often are case studies for creative approaches to section. From Herzog & de Meuron's Prada Aoyama to Kengo Kuma & Associates' Asakusa Culture and Tourism Center, the basic strategy of vertical stacking is challenged and complicated by alternative sectional interventions. Shaped volumes containing changing rooms are nested within the stacked levels of the Prada department store, all enclosed in a shaped box or volume. In Kuma's design, individual shaped forms containing nested volumes within volumes, complete with inclined floors, are placed on top of one another to form a tower.

Complex public or cultural buildings are most often the site for sectional intricacy. These projects often include combinations of program-specific spaces that require the integration of discrete shapes or figures within a given envelope. Theaters, concert halls, and other performance spaces have stages and sloped auditoriums that figure prominently, requiring complementary circulation systems and support floors, as exemplified by OMA's Casa da Música. Similarly, multifunction academic and civic buildings, including Mack Scogin Merrill Elam Architects' Knowlton School of Architecture, OMA's Seattle Central Library, Álvaro Siza's Iberê Camargo Foundation Museum, Morphosis's 41 Cooper Square, NADAA's Melbourne School of Design, Diller Scofidio + Renfro's Museum of Image and Sound, and Grafton Architects' Università Luigi Bocconi, all use section to create inventive works of architecture that resolve complex programmatic assemblages.

By incorporating a range of distinct sectional approaches within a single building, these projects provide a rich source of study and investigation. While the works used to exemplify one type of section were selected because of their ability to clarify and distill a given approach, they do not always illustrate the spatial play of the hybrid combinations. The interplay of two or more approaches to section gives architects the capacity to not only accommodate complex programs but develop projects that are multilayered. This does not mean, though, that all projects that use more than one type of section are necessarily interesting or compelling works of architecture. Rather, the exploration of the variety and complexity of hybrid approaches demonstrates the expansive range of possibilities of the heuristic structure of section types. The classification system is used not to constrain but to catalyze architectural discourse.

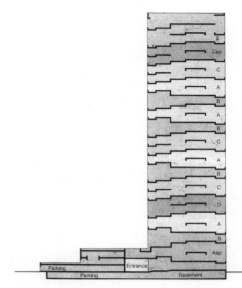

Charles Correa, Kanchanjunga Apartments, 1983

Excerpts from a History of Section

Given its extensive use in architectural practice today, the section arrives surprisingly late in the history of architectural drawing. In fact, while individual instances of sectional drawing were in evidence by the early part of the fifteenth century, section as a codified drawing type did not complete the triumvirate of plan, section, and elevation in European architectural academies and competitions until the late seventeenth or early eighteenth century.[12] While it is beyond the scope of this essay to map a comprehensive history of the architectural section over the course of the last several hundred years in the West, it's instructive to frame the major changes in the conceptualization and deployment of section in order to contextualize its current status and potential.

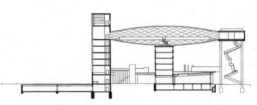

Steven Holl Architects, American Library Berlin, 1989

Mecanoo Architecten, Technical University Delft Library, 1997

What follows is a series of episodes that coalesce around several key ideas. Discontinuous and incomplete, these moments reveal the potentials and paradoxes of the section. Primary among these contradictions is the dual nature of the term *section* itself. When we speak about section we mean both a representational technique and a series of architectural practices pertaining to the vertical organization of buildings and related architectural and urbanistic constructions. These conditions are interrelated both historically and professionally. Although the two meanings of the term are often used interchangeably and fluidly, we will attempt to clarify this relationship in order to examine the historical trajectory of the section, from its origins as a representational mode to its development as a set of design practices with spatial, tectonic, and performative implications.

THE ANALYTICAL CUT: ARCHAEOLOGY AND ANATOMY

The origin of section as a representational mechanism, while obscure, has typically been associated with its capacity to reveal the hidden workings of an existing building or body—often as a retrospective or analytical technique. The earliest surviving

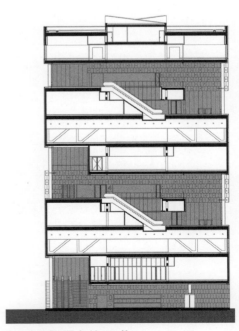

Neutelings Riedijk Architects, Museum aan de Stroom, 2010

Villard de Honnecourt, Reims Cathedral, ca. 1230

Donato Bramante, Roman ruins, ca. 1500

Giuliano da Sangallo, Temples of Portumnus and Vesta, 1465

Leonardo da Vinci, study for central plan church, ca. 1507

drawings that tentatively depict conditions of an architectural section are Villard de Honnecourt's parchment studies of medieval cathedrals from the thirteenth century.[13] Among the sixty-three pages of his known drawings, which range broadly in subject matter, are hints of a cut through the exterior wall of Reims Cathedral, shown to the side of a drawing primarily intended to illustrate the sequence of flying buttresses shown in elevation. Indeed, while Honnecourt's drawing is orthogonal and made through clean lines, the section as a cut is tentative and incomplete, acting as a side note to the depiction of structural complexities that merge with the qualities of the architecture in the Gothic cathedral. Nevertheless, this early example presages one of the predominant uses of the sectional drawing—as a means to analyze and represent structural and constructional relationships visible only through the delineation of a building's vertical organization.

While Honnecourt's drawing suggests that section was not wholly unknown in architectural circles prior to the Renaissance, its rise as a codified form of representation has been linked to two related precursors that originate from outside architecture proper: the observation of archaeological ruins and the biological description of the human body.[14] In both instances, section is explicitly associated with the visual and physical dissection of an extant body, whether constructed or organic. As such, section originates as the drawn record of an observed material condition first and as a representational mechanism only in retrospect.

Jacques Guillerme and Hélène Vérin's article "The Archaeology of Section" traces the origin of the architectural drawing to the observation and subsequent depiction of Roman ruins and to the physical breaks and discontinuities in decaying structures.[15] These fragmented monuments provided a view that simultaneously exposed interior and exterior to the eye of the touring architect or artist. According to Guillerme and Vérin, the practice of recording through drawing these surviving monuments in their state of romantic decay gave slow birth to the section as a conscious projection of architectural intentionality, "transforming the observation of archaeological remains into the observance of architectural diagrams." The section understood as an imaginary cut through an otherwise solid building or as a means of describing a future construction comes only after the documentation of ruins that reveal what would otherwise be hidden. This translation necessitated a conceptual shift from a literal depiction of a fragmented building to an abstract device: the imaginary plane of the sectional cut. The conventional nature of this transformation is recorded in the variety of techniques used to make explicit the operations of the cut, ranging from the device of rendering new or projected buildings in quasiruined form to the emergence of poché as a method for depicting the conceptually solid structural fabric of a building.

A parallel set of antecedents can be found in artistic and scientific practices depicting the body and its internal organs that evolved from the physical dissection of human remains and from investigative anatomy as it emerged in the fifteenth century. As with the architectural section, these drawings often relied upon an inventive array of visual devices to render explicit the sectional nature of the cuts. The most often cited are Leonardo da Vinci's obsessive studies of the human form, including his drawing of a human skull, which combines aspects of plan, elevation, and section in a cutaway perspective. Leonardo's depiction of a cranium was not unlike that of the dome in his contemporaneous study for a circular library, both demonstrating the act of cutting as essential to simultaneously show exterior and interior conditions of the body or building.

In perhaps the most famous of these early medical examples, Andreas Vesalius's *De Humani Corporis Fabrica* (1543), the variously skinned and flayed bodies are depicted in poses that mimic those of living and allegorical subjects. These woodcut illustrations are intricately constructed, not only to display the internal structure of muscles and viscera but also to acknowledge the act of cutting as both a physical operation and a representational conceit. Figures adopt stances that help to demonstrate the anatomical systems on view—but also fancifully seem to participate in their own dissection and display.

While it may be difficult to verify any causal relation between these biological depictions and architectural practice, it is nonetheless possible to identify productive similarities whereby techniques applied in one sphere reappeared in the other, suggesting a cross-fertilization of graphic techniques and modes of representation. More important, however, drawing techniques derived from both archaeological and anatomical practices strongly indicate that section originated as a retrospective rather than prospective tool, an analytical device rather than a generative instrument. It is perhaps this origin in the recording and revealing of extant conditions that has accounted for the slow integration of section as a productive instrumentality in architectural practice.

THE EMERGENCE OF THE ARCHITECTURAL SECTION: MEASURE AND PERCEPTION

Sectional drawing as an explicitly architectural technique appears in the work of Italian architects in the latter half of the fifteenth century. At this time a renewed interest in documenting the sectional ruins of classical antiquity intersected with the use of section for speculating on the structural and material properties of ancient buildings that had not deteriorated, as well as for describing new constructions and projects. The Pantheon, built by Emperor Hadrian in AD 128, was a frequent subject of inspired conjecture, with speculative section drawings executed in the hope of ascertaining the structural and proportional logic that had kept it intact.[16] It offered to architects a powerful subject for the use of section, given the seductive cut in the illuminating central oculus of the dome. Instead of a sealed dome, the Pantheon displayed a provocative void, allowing interior and exterior space to merge in a manner that would typically be seen only through a section drawing.

Early collections of Renaissance drawings (such as the *Codex Coner*, the *Codex Barberini*, and the sketches of Baldassarre

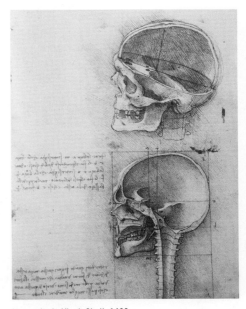

Leonardo da Vinci, Skull, 1489

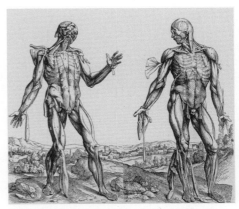

Andreas Vesalius, drawings, from *De Humani Corporis Fabrica*, 1543

Bernardo della Volpaia, Pantheon, from *Codex Coner*, ca. 1515

Bernardo della Volpaia, Tempietto, from *Codex Coner*, ca. 1515

Giuliano da Sangallo, centralized building, from *Codex Barberini*, ca. 1500

Antonio da Sangallo the Younger, St. Peter's, ca. 1520

Peruzzi) contain numerous sections, including different interpretations of the Pantheon as well as views of contemporaneous centralized churches. These drawings seek, through an imaginary cut, to trace the exterior and interior profile of the wall, thus visualizing the relationship between the building's form and the space it contained. Even in these early drawings the status of the section as a form of architectural representation was in question, as the mapping of the substance of the wall was only a part of the image. As Wolfgang Lotz noted in his essay "The Rendering of the Interior in Architectural Drawings of the Renaissance," section drawings developed not as a singular and fully codified practice but as a series of incipient operations that overlap and combine in promiscuous ways.[17] For Lotz, the question was less the status of the section cut itself than the role this drawing type was to play in either staging interior scenes or recording architectural measure and proportion. In the *Codex Coner* (a drawing set now attributed to Bernardo della Volpaia and dated to the early 1500s) the view within the sectioned walls is depicted through a single-point perspective. This painterly approach sacrifices dimensional accuracy for the illusion of a scene visible beyond the cut plane of the section. In contrast, certain sections in the *Codex Barberini* (attributed to Giuliano da Sangallo) and in the Pantheon drawing by Peruzzi demonstrate a commitment to orthographic projection, where the space beyond the cut is shown in elevation with no vanishing point or perspectival distortion.

While explicitly spatial, the sectional perspectives of the *Codex Coner* represent a highly particular notion of space, both adapted to and in part determined by the logic of the drawing type itself. The architectural historian and critic Robin Evans has argued that the inherent logic of the section drawing is heavily biased toward bilaterally symmetrical and axial spatial organizations, which are readily depicted through this technique.[18] Moreover, the centralized and frontal sections of the *Codex Coner* imply an understanding of space that is conceived volumetrically but also from the perspective of a static observer taking in the architecture as a pictorial composition. In this reading the perspectival section reinforces a notion of architecture as a principally optical phenomenon, and one tethered to a fixed viewpoint.

By contrast, in later drawings of the *Codex Barberini* and the work of Peruzzi and Antonio da Sangallo the Younger, the observer is progressively removed as a subject through the use of more orthogonal representational conventions in the depiction of section. These drawings abandon the optical distortions of perspective, resulting in a technique that can eliminate the subjective in favor of objective accuracy. This can be understood as a necessary development of the section drawing as a professional document, capable of conveying in unambiguous terms the dimensional and geometric information required by the builder. It is significant that this transition coincided with Sangallo's and Peruzzi's participation in the *fabricca* of St. Peter's under Raphael and the emergence of new hierarchies of building production that separated the architect from building. In Lotz's view this shift also leads to the possibility of more complex, dynamically conceived spaces, no longer restricted by the single static observation point of the *Codex Coner*.

Lotz makes a claim of evolutionary teleology from the earlier perspectival practices to the emergence of the strictly orthographic section. The perspectival section is principally an illustrative practice, one that maximizes the visual appeal of a singular image to convey both profile and space and combines the quantifiable with the perceptual. The orthographic section, on the other hand, is an instrument of metric description connected to the emergence of codified forms of construction documentation. However, its increase in accuracy requires a multiplication of drawings to provide the requisite information to comprehend complex spaces and architectural assemblies, as the absence of illusionistic depth flattens the legibility of spatial relationships.

This progressive bifurcation of orthographic section drawing from perspectival practices coincides with architecture's increasing divergence as a discipline from the other fine arts during the sixteenth century, as exemplified in the work of Sebastiano Serlio. The increasing use of the dimensionally accurate orthographic section, complete with notations of construction logic, parallels the emergence of the professional architect as distinct from the master craftsman. Whereas elevations describe the image and composition of architecture, a section is an instrument of instruction, conveying to the builder the means and profile of erection. Of the three primary orthographic drawing types—plan, elevation, and section—it is section that aligns most closely to structural and material designations. The typical orthographic section is in many ways the most sophisticated, combining in one image two types of representation: the objective profile marking the cut and the interior elevation beyond, describing the inhabitable space made possible by the inscribed wall.[19]

The section's place in the standard repertoire of orthographic representations is in clear evidence by the time Andrea Palladio's *Four Books of Architecture* was published in 1570.[20] Here building sections are paired with exterior elevations, each drawing type describing only half of the building and aligned through the use of only orthographic information. Interior perspectives that might better convey the experience of the work are suppressed in favor of measurable facts, reinforcing the conception of the architect as the organizer of geometry. The symmetry of Palladio's work enables this efficiency, which reduces the number of engravings necessary to illustrate a building completely. With this pairing the exterior elevation sits in juxtaposition to the interior elevation, the section serving to reveal the interplay between the shell of the building and its interior disposition. In Palladio's work the distinction and similarity between the section and the elevation are deployed to full effect. While sharing the profile of the building, the elevation illustrates the composition and order of architecture, legacies of architecture as an aesthetic art. Section reveals the material and mass necessary to construct the edifice, knowledge unique to architecture as a profession aligned with the craft of building. Palladio's section-elevation hybrids exemplify the dual nature of architecture as an art and a craft and illustrate the

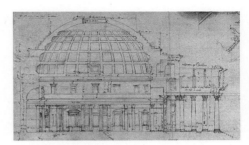

Baldassarre Peruzzi, Pantheon, 1531–35

Sebastiano Serlio, Project N13, from Book VII of *On Domestic Architecture*, ca. 1545

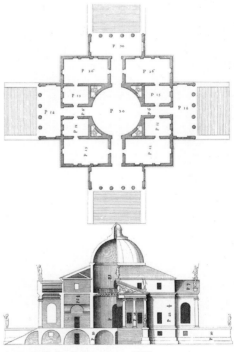

Andrea Palladio, La Rotonda, ca. 1570

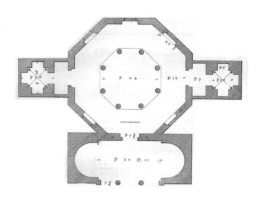

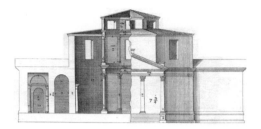

Andrea Palladio, baptisterium of Constantine, 1570

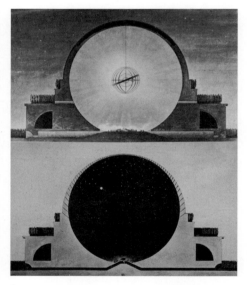

Étienne-Louis Boullée, cenotaph for Isaac Newton, 1784

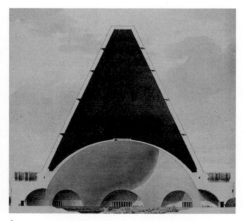

Étienne-Louis Boullée, conical cenotaph, ca. 1780

synthesis of the exterior and interior as quintessentially the domain of the architect.

It is important to note that the load-bearing obligation of the wall meant that for Palladio and his contemporaries, the shapes of the wall, floor, and ceiling were coincident with the structural system. Yet if we compare the plan and the section, the very same wall is rendered in completely opposite ways. In plan, walls are solid, filled in to reinforce the legibility of the organization of rooms and spaces, which are left blank. The walls in section are white, left as voids between the highly articulated interior surfaces beyond. The plan is the privileged architectural figure, with alignment between wall and spatial concept heavily marked. On a page, the plan dominates, setting the primary terms by which the building as an architectural composition is to be read and understood. In contrast, the material condition of the wall in section is left as a void, a gap between rooms. While the plan may organize, the section affords greater play among the shape, form, and organization of the material being cut and the inhabitable architectural space framed by it. Ceilings curve to disperse gravitational load over the large volumes; invisible roof trusses are given the same weight as the floor of the piano nobile; and the scale and size of each building are most clearly evident in section. It is the particular instrumentality of the section that allows for the simultaneous registration of both form and effect, providing a unique means for exploring, testing, and understanding complex interactions and exchanges of material and space.

ÉTIENNE-LOUIS BOULLÉE: FORM AND EFFECT

Nearly two hundred years after Palladio, the section drawing continued to increase in importance as a comprehensive means for conveying architectural effects, even though structural obligations remained consistent. It is perhaps in the unbuilt scheme of Étienne-Louis Boullée for the cenotaph for Isaac Newton of 1784 where section is deployed in full, illustrating its potential to choreograph the relationship among architecture, human inhabitants, and site. While Boullée's project was depicted in plan, elevation, and section, it is sectional drawings that convey the full force of the project. Two sections, one depicting daytime and the other night, capture fully the experiential inversion intended by the design. During the day, the interior of the massive sphere would be illuminated by cuts through the exterior walls, creating the impression of a captured night sky. At night, the inverse would occur, with a massive illuminated orb transforming the interior space into a daylit room.

Only through section drawings is the temporal juxtaposition between the constructed world within the architectural sphere and the natural world outside made visible. While the materiality of the building is never revealed, the tonal marking of the foundation, walls, and shell shifts to align with the pictorial goal of each section. A light section tone in the daytime image reveals conical cuts that penetrate the massive structure to create the illusion of night, whereas in the nighttime image, the section blends into the evening sky, retreating from consideration in deference to the power of the manufactured light source. Despite the absence of any perspectival projection, Boullée's section clearly demonstrates the capacity to convey experience over tectonic designation, aligning with his conviction that architecture should not be bound by obligations of building but premised on the embodiment of ideas. Paradoxically, section, the very drawing type now most associated with the materials of construction, was deployed by Boullée for the opposite purpose, illustrating succinctly its multivalent potential.

EUGENE EMMANUEL VIOLLET-LE-DUC: STRUCTURE AND EXPRESSION

In large part, constructions through the seventeenth century consisted of space circumscribed by masonry mass, resulting in sectional depictions in which exterior profile and interior space were closely interrelated through the thickness of the poche. However, during the eighteenth and nineteenth centuries, the solid wall of load-bearing masonry architecture was challenged by an increasingly layered set of conditions, reflecting new structural technologies associated with the emerging materials of cast and wrought iron. In this context the section gained enhanced currency as an effective means for describing and analyzing architectural form, understood as a direct expression of static forces. Of particular significance in this regard are the writings and drawings of the French architect and theorist Eugène-Emmanuel Viollet-le-Duc, who relied on the section to demonstrate the interdependency of formal and structural systems that were not only central to his ideas but key tenets in the development of modern architecture.

Viollet-le-Duc set his work in direct juxtaposition to the teachings of the École des Beaux-Arts, which had focused on composition and plan. In his *Lectures on Architecture*, Viollet-le-Duc outlined his goal to rethink Gothic architecture in order to adapt what he saw as its exemplary structural rationality to the new materials and constructional potentials of his time.[21] The *Lectures* are an expression of principles derived from the practices of previous eras, illustrated with sectional engravings. Rather than describing buildings per se, Viollet-le-Duc presented these engravings as a series of case studies that translate the masonry-based architecture of the past into the new expression proper to the nineteenth century. Viollet-le-Duc's comparative rendering in "Lecture XII" of medieval and modern methods for supporting a projecting gallery, for example, depicts the replacement of heavy stone corbeling by an iron strut. The efficacy of this methodology is described in the language of efficiency and economy: he writes, "We shall effect a saving in expense and shall obtain a building that will present greater security, will be less weighty, and will allow a better circulation of air about the ground floor."[22] His ideas are supported by the didactic nature of the section and its capacity to convey economically the dynamics of structural and other gravitational forces, from drainage to ventilation, in their relation to built form.

A related drawing by Viollet-le-Duc, from the same lecture, depicting a "novel method of resisting the thrust of vaulting,"

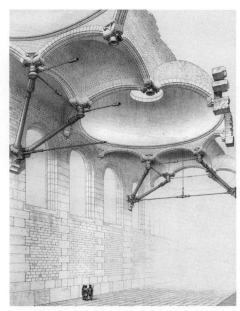

Eugène-Emmanuel Viollet-le-Duc, vaulted room, 1872

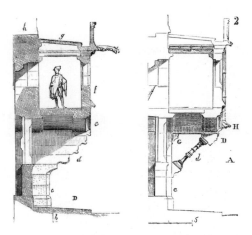

Eugène-Emmanuel Viollet-le-Duc, medieval and modern methods for supporting a projecting gallery, 1872

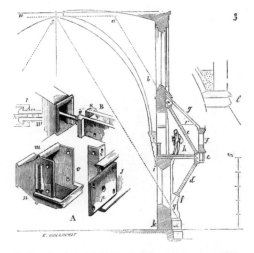

Eugène-Emmanuel Viollet-le-Duc, structural system, 1872

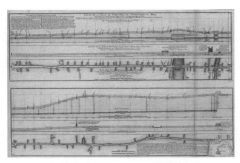

Phillipe Bauche, Coupe de la Ville de Paris, 1742

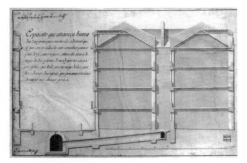

Eugénio dos Santos, street section, 1758

Pierre Patte, street section, 1769

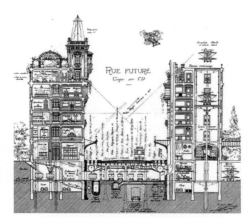

Eugène Hénard, illustration of the "Street of the Future," 1911

offers another example of section as a didactic and projective tool. Addressing the problem of the flying buttress, Viollet-le-Duc replaces the masonry mass of the Gothic buttress with a system of oblique iron struts, bars, and plates intended to resist the outward thrust of the masonry arches above. Importantly, the drawing includes not only the physical form of the new hybrid construction but also the geometry of its structural relationships, thus transcribing both the material and immaterial into a single representation to demonstrate the isomorphism between structural logic and architectural expression. Significantly, in none of these instances does Viollet-le-Duc provide a plan, as the principles involved relate primarily to the vertical dimension, where gravitational forces and static relationships hold sway.

These drawings also capitalize on the capacity of the section to reveal the constructional condition of the building as an assembly of constituent parts. Only through section could Viollet-le-Duc visualize the new architectural conditions he espoused: "We no longer have, as in Roman architecture, concrete and homogeneous masses, but rather a kind of organism whose every part has not only its purpose, but also an immediate action."[23] This shift from an architecture based on mass to one of discretely adapted parts prefigures the impact of industrialized production and the technologically driven constructional efficiencies that were to come to fruition in the twentieth century. It is also a conception of architecture that is effectively revealed through the device of the section. Since structural assemblies operate first and foremost in the vertical dimension, from foundation to column to arch to roof, the section displays these transferences of force and the corresponding building components in the most direct form. For Viollet-le-Duc, the section drawing becomes a transparent demonstration of the inevitability of architectural forms derived from the tectonic systems of new materials.

The adoption of industrialized construction techniques and materials changed fundamentally the nature of architectural practice, with the use of steel and iron columnar and long-span systems uncoupling the enclosure wall from structural obligations. Paradoxically, the same technological advances that made possible this interdependence of structure and form announced by Viollet-le-Duc set in motion the terms of their eventual disengagement within the modernist movement. The very efficiency of steel (and subsequently concrete) construction systems, which allowed them to work independently from exterior form and interior space, placed the section, understood as both a representational technique and a location of architectural practice, in a simultaneous point of liberation and crisis. The section, freed from alignment with structural forces, could take on a new role in regard to the manipulation of space. Simultaneously, the section's responsibility was challenged by the proliferation of repetitive columnar systems and concrete slabs, removing for all but long-span projects the obligation to sculpt gravitational forces through section as a driver of design. Freedom of form came through the loss of the structural or tectonic imperative that had previously informed the logic of section.

THE SECTIONAL CITY

With the growth of the metropolis that accompanied rapid industrialization, section evolved as a critical tool for understanding an increasingly complex layering of architectural, transportational, and hydrological systems. With urban density came the need for a network of interconnected systems to deliver the various services of the modernizing city. While master plans provided the means for organizing territory, allowing, for instance, the mapping of Manhattan's grid or the reworking of Paris's streets, boulevards, and parks, it was through the use of the urban cross-section that the increasingly important, yet invisible, operations of the city could not only be made visible but projected as an expansion of political control. Executed not as a recording of existing conditions but as a speculative image of the future, the street section demonstrates the power of this mode of representation to orchestrate divergent systems, opening new conceptual and spatial territory for development.

The drawings of the Portuguese engineer Eugénio dos Santos and those of the French engineer Pierre Patte are considered the earliest uses of section to organize and understand the metropolis conceived as a set of interconnected infrastructural systems.[24] Of the two, Patte's work is better known, given its influential role in transforming Paris. Executed in the 1760s, his urban plans and drawings proposed changes to the city and used section to demonstrate the integration of the inner workings of buildings, engaging the depth of the street as a site of future civic improvements.[25] Here the section reveals and organizes systems, unifying the interior of dwellings with the vast network of a shared waste system. Patte's drawings link the civic machinery of the waterworks with the interiors of the adjacent apartment buildings, suggesting the intimate connections between individual domestic lives and the sanitary infrastructure that ties them to larger urban networks. It is only through the use of the section that these two divergent aspects of the city can be understood and visualized as one system, obscuring boundaries of ownership and civic authority through the logic of the drawing. Patte gave greatest focus to the integration of building and street drainage into a shared collection tube, paying careful attention to the depth and materiality of the sewer to ensure the proper durability, slope, and water flow. By contrast, the architecture above the basement level is left blank, undifferentiated, and underdeveloped, a placeholder designating only future inhabitation. The street monument in the distance is given more attention than the buildings in section. As such, the design concept of Patte illustrates the two distinct trajectories of the urban section, one representing the increased complexity and layering of the city and the other the density made possible by an architecture of repetitive stacking.

Presented in 1910, Eugène Hénard's "The Cities of the Future" draws directly on the precedent set by Patte.[26] Hénard continued to use section to stitch together visible and unseen operations. Apprehending the challenges cities faced with the promise and potential of new transportation systems, he envisioned the city as a multilayered matrix of tunnels, tracks, and elevated railroads

Grand Central Terminal, New York, published in the *Scientific American*, 1912

Harvey Wiley Corbett, "City of the Future," 1913

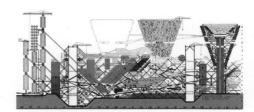

Peter Cook / Archigram, Plug-in City, Max Pressure Area, 1964

Chicago Central Area Transit Planning Study, 1968

33

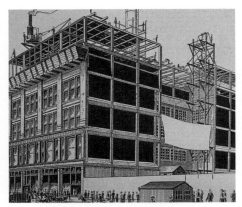

William Le Baron Jenney, Fair Store, 1891

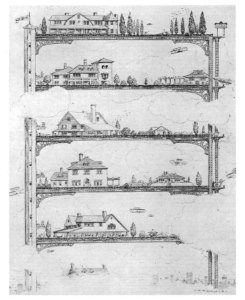

A. B. Walker, cartoon in *Life* magazine, March 1909

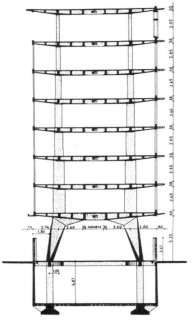

Pier Luigi Nervi, UNESCO Headquarters, 1958

that used section to thicken the very ground of the urban condition. Here coal carts render visible the connections among individual buildings and new infrastructural systems to provide power and energy. Amid exuberant embellishments such as vertical shafts to lift personal flying devices and automobiles, Hénard draws a series of stacked domestic spaces, ordinary and repetitive, capped in height only to allow sunlight to reach adjacent buildings.

Section drawings were instrumental in the thinking of modernist planners and architects like Hénard, as they transformed the ground into a foundation for a densely layered metropolis, accommodating emerging and often competing technologies of transportation and communication through distinct strata. The use of section was essential to the conceptualization of the city to come. From Corbett's City of the Future (1913) to plans for Grand Central Terminal in New York (1912) to Le Corbusier's Ville Radieuse (1924), visions of the future were coincident with the image of the city as a multilevel stage, thus leveraging section's capacity to hold in opposition contrasting or even contradictory programmatic conditions in a single view or space.

HEGEMONY OF THE STACK

While the infrastructures of the city have grown in complexity, from the eighteenth-century emphasis on hygiene and health to the twentieth-century commitment to transportation, power, and communication distribution, the section has continued to perform a significant role in the conceptualization of urban life. With the rise of populations living in closer proximity and in tighter quarters, section has become increasingly a means to organize and control the politics of the city, mapping the complex layers that are necessary to build and maintain urban systems. As unclaimed ground is increasingly at a premium, the section of cities becomes multilayered and contested, providing a ripe site for design projection and invention. From underground transportation and sewers to military and civilian shelters for survival, the infrastructure of industrialized cities of the late nineteenth and twentieth centuries was configured through sectional projection.

The population density that defines the modern metropolis is made possible only through the most banal forms of the architectural section, yet gives rise to the use of section as a means to legislate urban politics and map systemic control below- and above ground. Contemporary urban planning through zoning (including setback obligations and limits and controls on height) curbs the unchecked expansion of the city through sectional repetition. Whether through floor-to-area regulations, height restrictions, or sky-plane exposure analysis, contemporary zoning operates significantly through the control of section. Zoning controls often have introduced new imperatives for sectional invention in architecture. The 1916 New York zoning code gave direct rise to the ziggurat-shaped buildings of the 1930s, where a maximum vertical height was coupled with an upper-building envelope dictated by a plane drawn at an angle from the ground to ensure that light would penetrate to the street. Such edicts resulted in buildings whose sections were sheared and staggered, stepping back from the sidewalk to maximize enclosed space. Contemporary rules specifying that only certain types of spaces must be restricted according to floor-to-area ratios have led to inventive uses of section that skillfully deploy mezzanines, voids, and double-height spaces to maximize returns on architecture commodified as investment.

New urban building types increasingly have used sections as explanatory documents to catalog the multiplicity of systems, circulation paths, and programs that characterize department stores, multistage theaters, hotels, and train stations. The sophistication of building technology able to facilitate divergent uses in a constrained urban block was matched by the increasing use of section to pack often unrelated parts into a single shell or volume. These large-scale projects, often public in nature, incorporate the complex technical systems of the city within the space of a single structure and stand in direct contrast to the standardization of the section characteristic of private development. Yet at the core, all vertical buildings share a dependence on the elevator and other robust mechanical systems, without which multivalent and layered buildings would not be feasible.

The efficiencies of modern construction that have enabled urban densification have played a central role in the development of section. From the Chicago frame to the Dom-ino system, contemporary vertical building processes align perfectly with capitalism's driving obligation of creating maximum marketable area on a given plot of land for the least amount of cost. These systems of efficiency, now normative and nearly unquestioned, are in tension with the more intricate spatial types required to meet a variety of uses and building performances and negate the rich potential of more inventive sectional approaches. Not every human activity or building system is ideally served by the undifferentiated space provided by repetitive floor plates. It is precisely section drawing's aptness as a tool for imagining alternative ways of creating space that makes it a critical means of confronting dominant systems of construction and spatial organizations determined by systems of economic efficiencies. Given the environmental and human costs of the relentless pursuit of capital in so much of today's built environment, there is clearly a broad social and political potential in the exploration of more complex sectional practices.

THE CONTEMPORARY SECTION

The advances in material and structural systems of industrialization, combined with the economic imperatives of capitalism, have polarized the architecture of the twentieth and twenty-first centuries in relation to the section. At one end, efficiencies of economy push toward repetition and sameness. Simultaneously, the plasticity of construction materials and systems under the obligation to meet increasingly complex building requirements encourages a wider range of sectional exploration than what was possible with premodern load-bearing wall systems.

The interplay between standardization and complexity frames to a great degree the current approach to the conceptualization

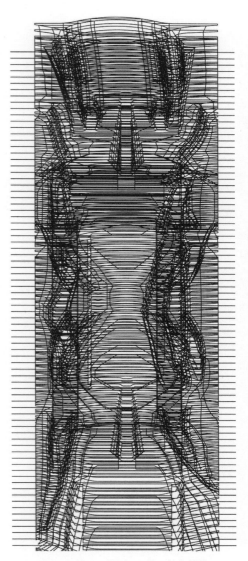

Foreign Office Architects, Yokohama Terminal, 2002

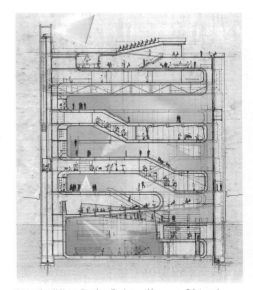

Diller Scofidio + Renfro, Eyebeam Museum of Art and Technology, 2004

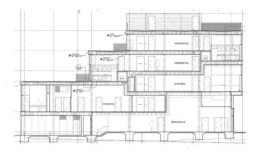

Höweler + Yoon Architecture, Building 2345, 2008

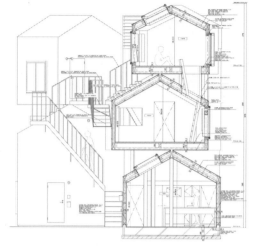

Sou Fujimoto, Tokyo Apartment, 2009

WORKac, Nature-City, 2012

of section in architectural discourse, informed in parallel by the fundamental shift over the last thirty years to the use of digital technology. The ability of computer-aided drawing programs to copy and paste with speed plays directly into economies of sameness. At the same time, digital modeling software programs have unleashed spatial, formal, and material complexities that were heretofore difficult, if not impossible, to visualize and realize, creating the possibility for unprecedented sectional complexity. The ability to cut or take a section through a three-dimensional model with speed has heightened the possibility to use section as a tool to inform the design process. Just as architects can use software to create and visualize complex forms, engineers can use computation to calculate loads and forces with the speed and certainty needed to ensure their structural integrity.

In turn, the ease of the section process establishes a means to translate between digital space and material form. For instance, closely spaced sections taken in parallel are often used to break larger forms and spaces into discrete pieces that can be cut, printed, or made and then reassembled to realize the whole. This sectioning process is widespread in practice and has, in turn, become a recognizable, even clichéd, aesthetic.[27] Yet the section cut is too often underused as a generative tool. In part, this is because the section is conceived as a software command, one among many built into the interface of the program. As such, section goes from being a site for invention to a resultant of the design process—the by-product of a visualization instruction.

The discourse of architecture at the opening of the twenty-first century has, however, been witness to discernible trends in the approach to section that highlight tendencies toward formal complexity. These recognizable practices are often the result of accommodating the increasingly dense programmatic and performative obligations of projects, enabled in part by increasingly sophisticated data and computational software.

One identifiable approach is the stacking of nested sections of legible program-specific volumes or rooms (rather than floor plates) to compose an overall architectural figure. These buildings embrace the hegemony of the stack as a catalyst for experimentation. Designed with a playfulness akin to building with children's blocks, these structures include MVRDV's Market Hall in Rotterdam, where the stacking of living units into an arc through horizontal shear forms a public canopy over a sandwich of retail and parking below. Höweler + Yoon Architecture deploys a combination of nest and vertical shear to creatively intertwine apartments, working within site constraints.

Alternatively, practices have explored the stacking of highly figural nested shapes that often do not fit together neatly. The resulting section is an accumulation of figures set in tension with one another, where the individually shaped units remain discernible, as evident in WORKac's Nature-City project and Sou Fujimoto's Tokyo Apartment. In these designs, the accumulation of a range of distinct interior spaces and their qualities is coextensive with the logic of the exterior form.

Development of the incline section has resulted in two related sectional trends, one more interior and the other more exterior. In the interior incline section model, architects have sought to extend the sloped floor to align with the shape of entire projects. Such designs turn the now familiar fusing of an inclined floor and wall via a fillet into a total project, with complex topographies enveloping and engaging all surfaces. Here the utility of the inclined section is coupled with a fully three-dimensional figure of continuity. Given the cost and complexity of these projects, such an approach is usually associated with significant cultural destinations, exemplified by Toyo Ito's Taichung Metropolitan Opera House and Zaha Hadid's Abu Dhabi Performing Arts Centre. In a related trope, the section is used to merge building and landscape, with the inclined floor exaggerated and sculpted rhetorically to emphasize the blurred relationship.[28] In Steven Holl's Vanke Center, Snøhetta's Norwegian National Opera and Ballet, and Dominique Perrault's Ewha Womans University, portions of the buildings' roofs are merged with landscape, complicating expectations of the ground plane through sectional mating.

Our intent with this book is to create an open-ended and flexible approach to section that can serve as a shared basis for analysis and critical discussion of this undertheorized architectural design tool. By outlining the history of section and articulating clear differences among section types through the creation of a classification structure, we can understand and explore section more precisely and creatively. Indeed, the contemporary practice of architecture, organized and transformed by digital technology, is especially in need of tools to study and examine sections.

Section is the critical means for considering the social, environmental, and material questions of our current century. Designing and thinking through section establishes immediately a relationship among architectural form, interior space, and exterior site, where the consequences of scale are tangible and visceral. In the section, environmental and natural systems are described, engaged, and explored. Through section, the interplay of material invention and tectonic logic sets the stage for the framing of space and its use. As a cut into that which cannot be seen, the section embodies and reveals new territories for the continued architectural experimentation and exploration of our present future.

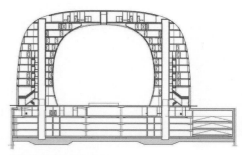

MVRDV, Market Hall, 2014

Zaha Hadid Architects, Abu Dhabi Performing Arts Center, 2008

Snøhetta, Norwegian National Opera and Ballet, 2008

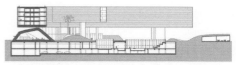

Steven Holl Architects, Vanke Center, 2009

1   Wolfgang Lotz, "The Rendering of the Interior in Architectural Drawings of the Renaissance," in *Studies in Italian Renaissance Architecture* (Cambridge, MA: MIT, 1977), 1–65.
2   Jacques Guillerme and Hélène Vérin, "The Archaeology of Section," *Perspecta* 25 (1989): 226–57.
3   Rem Koolhaas, *Delirious New York: A Retroactive Manifesto for Manhattan* (New York: Monacelli, 1994), 157.
4   In 2003 the building was converted to a condominium. The friction between a condominium, where maximizing the plan's square footage is paramount, and this idiosyncratic section—now void of its programmatic substantiation but still present as structure—produced interesting anomalies that were compounded by the facade's landmarked status.

5   For a detailed presentation of a range of shaped sections in ceilings see
    Farshid Moussavi, *The Function of Form* (Barcelona: Actar and Harvard
    University Graduate School of Design, 2009).

6   Colin Rowe, "The Mathematics of the Ideal Villa," in *The Mathematics of
    the Ideal Villa and Other Essays* (Cambridge, MA: MIT, 1982), 11. It is
    debatable exactly how Rowe would argue that Palladio's Malcontenta is
    a free section or what he precisely means by free section, as in the essay
    he elaborates little on it beyond associating it with volumetric modeling.

7   Herman Hertzberger, *Lessons for Students in Architecture* (Rotterdam:
    010, 1991), 202.

8   Hollywood's infatuation with using these spaces for action movies—
    witness *Die Hard, Mission Impossible, Sneakers, Speed, Salt,* and
    Inception—speaks to their visual seductiveness, as they induce vertigo
    and exploit zones that are not normally visible in most buildings.

9   The celebrated section of Le Corbusier's Unité d'Habitation is a stack of
    Citrohans. These are vertically mirrored, leaving a void in plan every third
    floor. The plan voids form a hallway that feeds to pairs of apartments on
    the three floors.

10 Despite Le Corbusier's claim in the *Oeuvre complète* that the Villa Savoye
    possesses a "very slight inclined ramp which leads almost imperceptibly
    to the upper level," this ramp exceeds the 1:12 slope stipulated by today's
    code. At the current ratio, it would take 120 feet of run, or 65 feet in a
    cut-back ramp with landings, to rise 10 feet.

11 In this light, the proliferation of projects in which inclined surfaces are
    extended from floors to walls through fillets can be seen as an attempt
    to make the continuity more legible, even if that continuity is largely
    rhetorical.

12 Guillerme and Vérin, "Archaeology of Section."

13 James S. Ackerman, *Origins, Imitations, Conventions* (Cambridge, MA:
    MIT, 2002). See also James S. Ackerman, "Villard de Honnecourt's
    Drawings of Reims Cathedral: A Study in Architectural Representation,"
    Artibus et Historae 18, no. 35 (1997): 41–49.

14 Robin Evans, *The Projective Cast: Architecture and Its Three Geometries*
    (Cambridge, MA: MIT, 2000), 118.

15 Guillerme and Vérin, "Archaeology of Section."

16 Tod A. Marder, "Bernini and Alexander VII: Criticism and Praise of the
    Pantheon in the Seventeenth Century," *Art Bulletin* 71 (1989): 628–45.

17 Lotz, "Rendering of the Interior."

18 Evans, *Projective Cast*, 118.

19 For more on the relationship between elevation, section, and perspective,
    see Evans, *Projective Cast*.

20 Andrea Palladio, *The Four Books on Architecture* (1570), trans. Richard
    Schofield and Robert Tavernor (Cambridge, MA: MIT, 2002).

21 Eugène Emmanuel Viollet-le-Duc, *Lectures on Architecture,* vol. 2 (1872),
    trans. Benjamin Bucknall (Boston: James R. Osgood and Co., 1881).
    See also Robin Middleton, "The Iron Structure of the Bibliothèque Sainte-
    Geneviève as the Basis of a Civic Decor," *AA Files* 40 (2000): 33–52.

22 Viollet-le-Duc, *Lectures on Architecture,* 56.

23 Viollet-le-Duc, *Lectures on Architecture,* 58.

24 Andrew J. Tallon, "The Portuguese Precedent for Pierre Patte's Street
    Section," *Journal of the Society of Architectural Historians* 63, no. 3
    (2004): 370–77.

25 Tallon, "Portuguese Precedent." Tallon argues that an earlier engineer,
    Eugenio dos Santos, was the first to design the urban section that influ-
    enced Patte.

26 Eugène Hénard, "The Cities of the Future," in *Transactions: Town Planning
    Conference, London, 10–15 October 1910* (London: Royal Institute of
    British Architecture, 1911), 345–67.

27 Lisa Iwamoto, "Sectioning," in *Digital Fabrications: Architectural and
    Material Techniques* (New York: Princeton Architectural Press, 2009),
    17–41.

28 Stan Allen and Marc McQuade, eds., *Landform Building* (Baden: Lars
    Müller, 2011).

BIBLIOGRAPHY

Ackerman, James S. "Architectural Practice in the Italian Renaissance." *Journal of the Society of Architectural Historians* 13, no. 3 (1954): 3–11.

Ackerman, James S. "Villard De Honnecourt's Drawings of Reims Cathedral: A Study in Architectural Representation." *Artibus et Historae* 18, no. 35 (1997): 41–49.

Allen, Stan, and Marc McQuade, eds. *Landform Building*. Baden: Lars Müller, 2011.

Ashby, Thomas. "Sixteenth-Century Drawings of Roman Buildings Attributed to Andreas Coner." *Papers of the British School of Rome* 2 (1904): 1–88.

Carlisle, Stephanie, and Nicholas Pevzner. *The Performative Ground: Rediscovering the Deep Section*, 2012, accessed October 15, 2014, http://scenariojournal.com/article/the-performative-ground/.

Chapman, Julia. "Paris: The Planned City in Section." Undergraduate thesis, Princeton University, 2009.

Emmons, Paul. "Immured: The Uncanny Solidity of Section." Paper presented at the Association of Collegiate Schools of Architecture, Montreal, Quebec, Canada, 2011.

Evans, Robin. *The Projective Cast: Architecture and Its Three Geometries*. Cambridge, Massachusetts: MIT, 2000.

Guillerme, Jacques, and Hélène Vérin. "The Archaeology of Section." *Perspecta* 25. Cambridge, Massachusetts: MIT, 1989.

Hénard, Eugène. "The Cities of the Future." In *Transactions: Town Planning Conference, London, 10–5 October 1910*, 345–67. London: Royal Institute of British Architecture, 1911.

Iwamoto, Lisa. *Digital Fabrications: Architectural and Material Techniques*. New York: Princeton Architectural Press, 2009.

Koolhaas, Rem. *Delirious New York: A Retroactive Manifesto for Manhattan*. New York: Monacelli, 1994.

Lewis, Paul, Marc Tsurumaki, and David J. Lewis. *Lewis.Tsurumaki.Lewis: Intensities*. New York: Princeton Architectural Press, 2013.

Lewis, Paul, Marc Tsurumaki, and David J. Lewis. *Lewis.Tsurumaki.Lewis: Opportunistic Architecture*. New York: Princeton Architectural Press, 2008.

Lotz, Wolfgang. *Studies in Italian Renaissance Architecture*. Cambridge, MA: MIT, 1977.

Machado, Rodolfo, and Rodolphe el-Khoury. *Monolithic Architecture*. New York: Prestel-Verlag, 1995.

Magrou, Rafaël. "The Glories of the Architectural Section." *Harvard Design Magazine* 35 (2012): 34–39.

Marder, Tod A. "Bernini and Alexander VII: Criticism and Praise of the Pantheon in the Seventeenth Century." *Art Bulletin* 71 (1989): 628–45.

Moussavi, Farshid. *The Function of Form*. Barcelona: Actar and Harvard University Graduate School of Design, 2009.

O'Neill, John P., ed. *Leonardo Da Vinci: Anatomical Drawings from the Royal Library Windsor Castle*. New York: Metropolitan Museum of Art, 1983.

Palladio, Andrea. *The Four Books on Architecture*. Translated by Richard Schofield and Robert Tavernor. Cambridge, MA: MIT, 2002.

Rohan, Timothy M. *The Architecture of Paul Rudolph*. New Haven: Yale University Press, 2014.

Rosenfeld, Myra Nan. *Serlio on Domestic Architecture*. Mineola, New York: Dover Publications, 1978.

Serlio, Sebastiano. *The Five Books of Architecture*. London: Robert Peake, 1611.

Tallon, Andrew J. "The Portuguese Precedent for Pierre Patte's Street Section." *Journal of the Society of Architectural Historians* 63, no. 3 (2004): 370–77.

Tsukamoto, Toshiharu, and Momoyo Kaijima. *Graphic Anatomy: Atelier Bow-Wow*. Minato City, Tokyo: TOTO, 2007.

Tsukamoto, Yoshiharu, and Momoyo Kaijima. *Graphic Anatomy 2: Atelier Bow-Wow*. Minato City, Tokyo: TOTO, 2014.

Viollet-le-Duc, Eugène Emmanuel. *Dictionnaire Raisonné De L'Architecture Française Du Xie Au Xvie Siècle*. 8 vols. Paris: Morel, 1858–68.

Viollet-le-Duc, Eugène Emmanuel. *Discourses on Architecture*. Translated by Henry Van Brunt. Vol. 1. Boston: James R. Osgood and Co., 1875.

Viollet-le-Duc, Eugène Emmanuel. *Lectures on Architecture*. Translated by Benjamin Bucknall. Vol. 2. Boston: James R. Osgood and Co., 1881.

The direct extrusion of a plan to a height
sufficient for the intended use

The layering of floors directly on top of one another; an extruded
section, repeated with or without variations

The deformation of one or more of the primary horizontal
surfaces of a building to sculpt space

The use of a rift or cut along either the horizontal or vertical axis
of a building to generate sectional difference

The deployment of any number or scale of penetrations through
a slab, exchanging lost floor area for benefits in section

The manipulation of the angle of an occupiable horizontal
plane, which tilts the plan into section

The creation of sectional consequences through
an interplay or overlap of legible volumes

Any combination of Stack, Extrusion, Shape, Shear, Hole, Incline,
and Nest; buildings rarely exhibit section types in isolation

The extrusion of a plan up to a height sufficient for the intended activity is the most basic form of a section. An extruded section has little to no variation in the vertical axis. The vast majority of buildings are based on this efficiency, including strip malls, big-box stores, factories, single-story houses, and the floors of most office, retail, and multistory residential buildings.

EXTRUSION

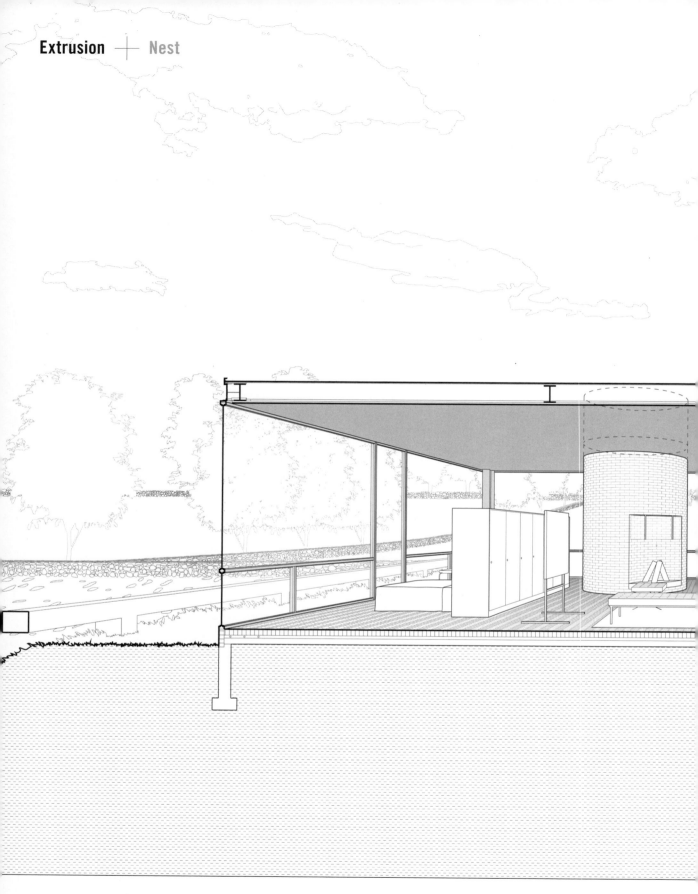

Glass House | New Canaan, Connecticut, USA

The first of fourteen structures built on his estate, Philip Johnson's Glass House is enclosed by a steel-framed ceiling standing 10 ft 6 in (3.2 m) above a brick floor on eight perimeter columns punctuating the window walls. The horizontal roof-spanning members are embedded within the smooth plane of the ceiling to render them invisible from within the house, leaving only the thin profile of the steel windows to frame large expanses of glass. Partial-height wood cabinets and a full-height cylinder of brick delineate the program of the house. The cabinets separate the bed from the open living

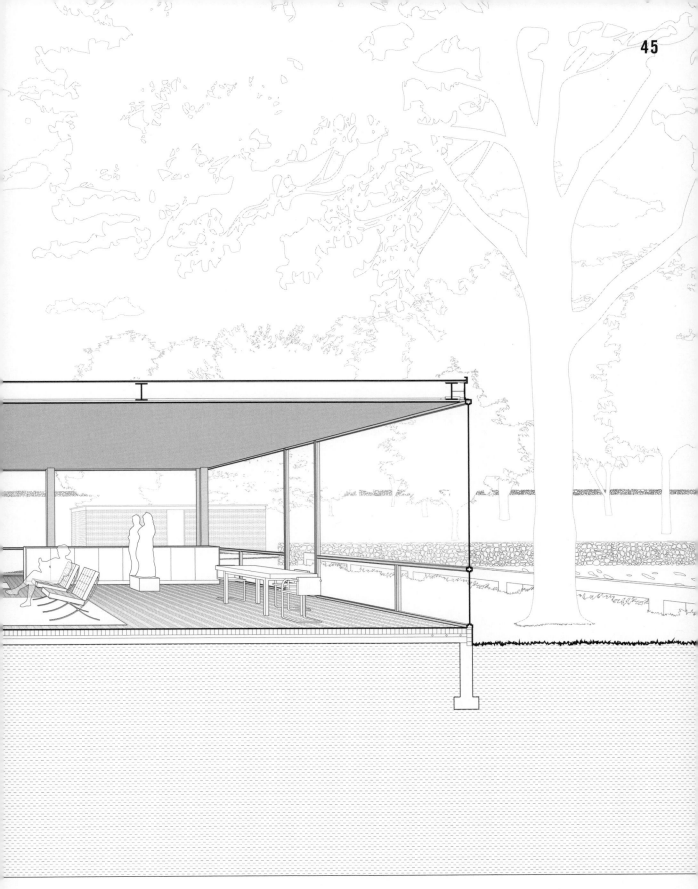

Philip Johnson | 1949

space, and the brick cylinder, extruding the brick floor into a vertical core, contains the bathroom and fireplace. As a consequence of the extruded section, the walls of glass generate visual exchanges—animated by light, reflections, weather, and seasonal variations—between the interior space and the more expansive landscapes surrounding the pavilion. Here the section induces horizontal rather than vertical visual effects.

Extrusion

Palace of Labor | Turin, Italy

Covering 269,098 sq ft (25,000 sq m), this enormous exhibition hall and training center was designed in part as a response to the expedited construction sequence of a competition. Built in eleven months, the roof was conceived as sixteen individual 82-ft-tall (25 m) mushroomlike forms, each consisting of a 65-ft-7-in (20 m) cast-in-place reinforced-concrete column topped with a 131-ft-3-in (40 m) square steel roof assembly. The accumulation of these units, built one by one, allowed interiors and the glass enclosure to be constructed prior to the completion of the entire roof. The large concrete

Pier Luigi Nervi | 1961

columns taper from a 16-ft-5-in-wide (5 m) cruciform, to a 8-ft-2-in-diameter (2.5 m) circle, to which are anchored twenty radiating steel-beam spokes that support the roof. Continuous glass strips run between the structures, allowing natural light into the space and registering the autonomy of each massive structural unit. A row of external steel ribs spans between a perimeter mezzanine and the roof to stiffen the enclosing glass curtain. The height and scale of this section exceeds conventions and transforms this extruded section into a grand civic space and spectacle.

Extrusion

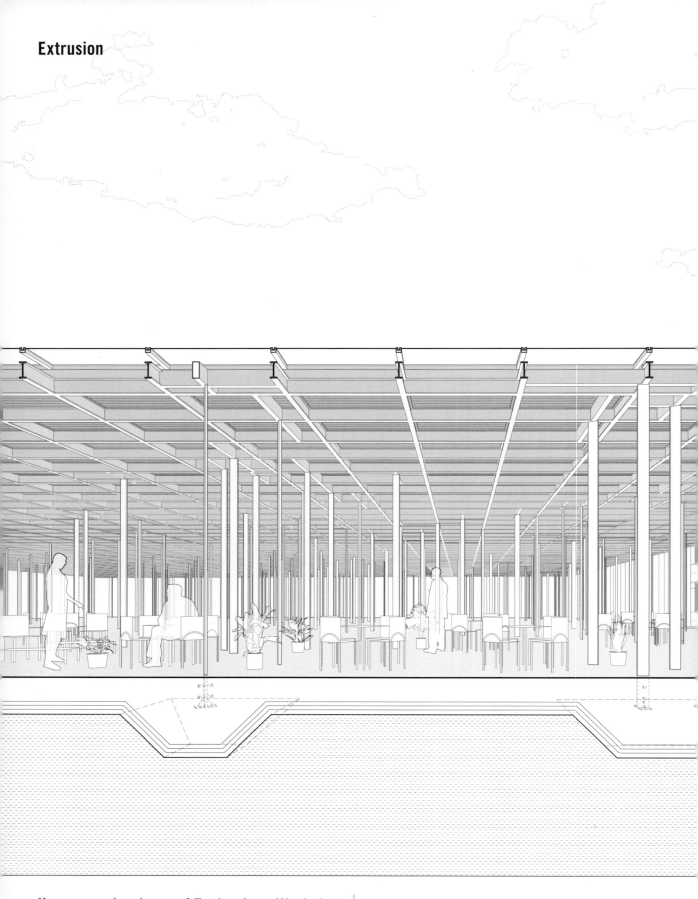

Kanagawa Institute of Technology Workshop | Kanagawa, Japan

In plan, this one-story space is configured as a slightly deformed square with 151-ft (46 m) sides. Steel columns (305 total) are distributed in clusters of varying densities to produce a range of flexible workshops for engineering students. The columns range in size from 5/8 by 5 3/4 in (1.6 by 14.5 cm) to 2 1/2 by 3 1/2 in (6.3 by 9.0 cm) and are painted white. Forty-two of these steel columns are in compression, and 263 are post-tensioned to withstand lateral forces. At a height of 16 ft 5 in (5 m), the roof is composed of a flat grid of 7 7/8-in-deep (20 cm) girders. The columns

Junya Ishigami + Associates | 2010

tether the roof down to a concrete slab with numerous footings. In contrast to extruded sections like those of big-box stores that reduce the quantity of columns to increase the efficiency and flexibility of the plan, the workshop transforms the vertical structure from a collection of single columns into a complex field, blurring distinctions between structure and space and producing difference rather than uniformity. The space of this extruded section is articulated by an approach to the vertical structure that redefines expectations of efficiency and hierarchy.

Stacking increases the real estate value of a property by expanding the square footage and programmatic capacity of a building without increasing its footprint. This is a basic motivation for the creation of section in architecture. A repetitive stack is largely an extruded section, deployed ad nauseam. By itself, stacking does not produce interior effects.

STACK

Stack

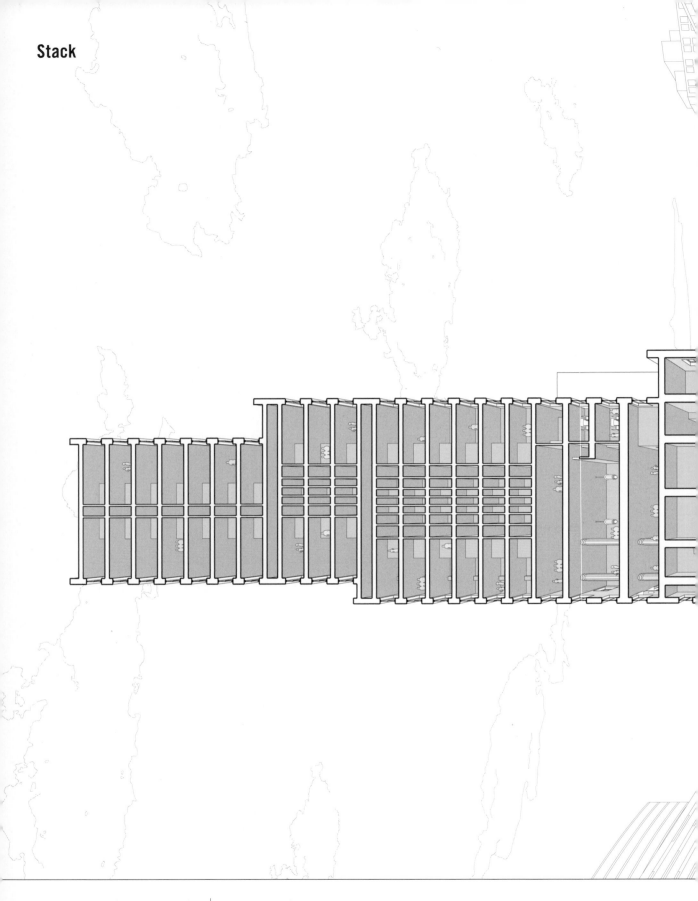

Downtown Athletic Club | New York, New York, USA

While the setback massing of the Downtown Athletic Club was a consequence of zoning regulations, the vertical blocks that it forms correspond to the stacking of interior programs. Lobbies, offices, and billiard rooms fill the widest block at the bottom. Most of the next block comprises athletic programs, each inhabiting its own full floor. Social programs, lounges, and dining rooms transition to the narrower top blocks, which contain smaller-scale bedrooms. Wide-span steel girders allow for a column-free space on the south side of each floor, with vertical circulation forming a linear core

Starrett & Van Vleck | 1930

on the north side of the building. There are nineteen different ceiling heights within the thirty-five levels, ranging from a 6-ft (1.8 m) "bedroom utility" to a 23-ft-6-in (7.2 m) "gymnasium." These variations in section are not revealed on the facade; they are experienced only through the elevator and stairs.

Because the stacked section maintains the autonomy of each floor and multiplies the area of the ground plane, a range of programs—many with the precise vertical dimension required by a particular sport—can coexist within a tight urban footprint.

S. R. Crown Hall | Chicago, Illinois, USA

As the central building in Mies van der Rohe's IIT campus, Crown Hall contains studio and exhibition space for the architecture school on its main floor, with offices, workrooms, and classrooms on the lower level. The unencumbered 220-by-120-ft (67.1 by 36.6 m) upper-level space is made possible by resting the four 6-ft-deep (1.8 m), welded double-plate girders on eight perimeter columns that are located outside of the interior space, effectively suspending the roof and ceiling. This produces a clear, 18-ft-high (5.5 m) interior space punctuated only by two ventilation shafts and oak partitions. To calibrate natural light and visual relationships

Ludwig Mies van der Rohe | 1956

with the outside, the window walls are treated differently on either side of a horizontal datum at 8 ft (2.4 m): above, venetian blinds cover transparent glass, while below 8 ft, the glass is translucent. Louvers at the base of the window walls provide natural ventilation. While the expansive, unitary space of this extruded section provides the spectacle of the building, this space is made possible by the utilitarian function of a partially submerged lower floor that contains additional classrooms, service spaces, and vertical circulation within cement-block walls. Crown Hall is an exuberant extruded section, supported by a pragmatic base.

Stack ─┼─ Hole

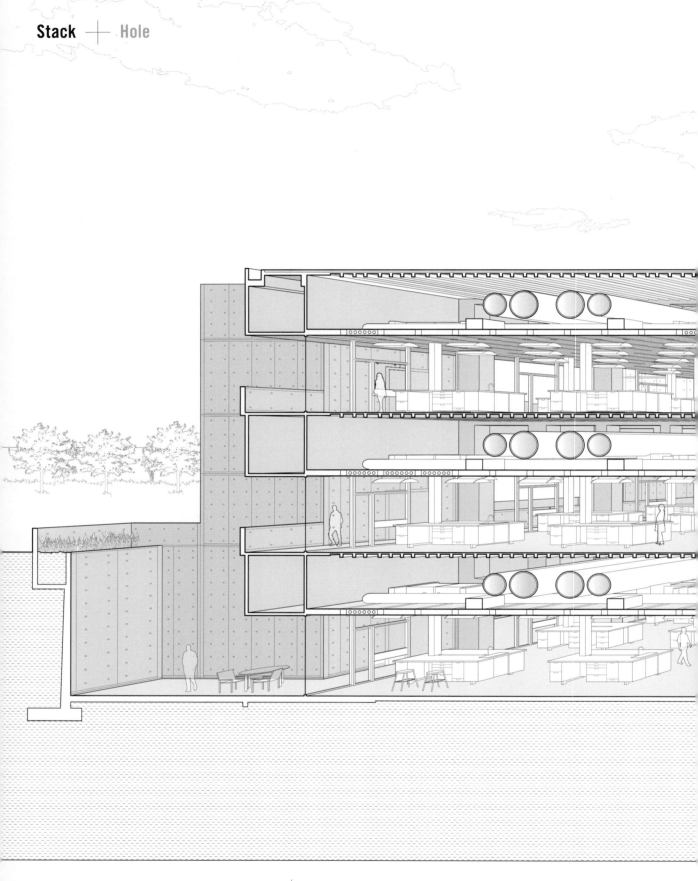

Salk Institute for Biological Studies | La Jolla, California, USA

Two sets of five towers symmetrically flank the Salk Institute courtyard. Each set of towers is connected to a laboratory building on the outer edge. The laboratories are column-free, 65-by-245-ft (19.8 by 74.7 m) spaces with 11-ft-3-in (3.4 m) ceilings. Poured-in-place concrete Vierendeel trusses span the width

of the laboratories and produce a floor above each laboratory for mechanical systems. Although there are only three levels of laboratories, the building is often said to be six stories, given the prominence of the service floors in the section. Due to local building-height limits, one-third of the building is located below

Louis I. Kahn | 1965

grade. On both sides of the laboratory buildings, large light wells bring daylight
to the lower levels. The dimensions of the laboratory buildings' stacked section
are consistent with the study towers, where the studios align with the service floors
to provide a separation between the studios and the laboratories.

São Paolo Museum of Art | São Paolo, Brazil

This cultural center comprises three stacked volumetric parts: the first suspended 26 ft 3 in (8 m) in the air, the second submerged below grade, and the third located in between—an exterior belvedere at street level. Two pairs of hollow prestressed 8-ft-2-in—by—11-ft-6-in (2.5 by 3.5 m) concrete frames span the 243-ft (74.1 m) length of the upper volume, suspending two floors. The lower floor contains offices, a library, and a central exhibition space, with circulation corridors located immediately below the concrete beam. On the upper level, the concrete beams

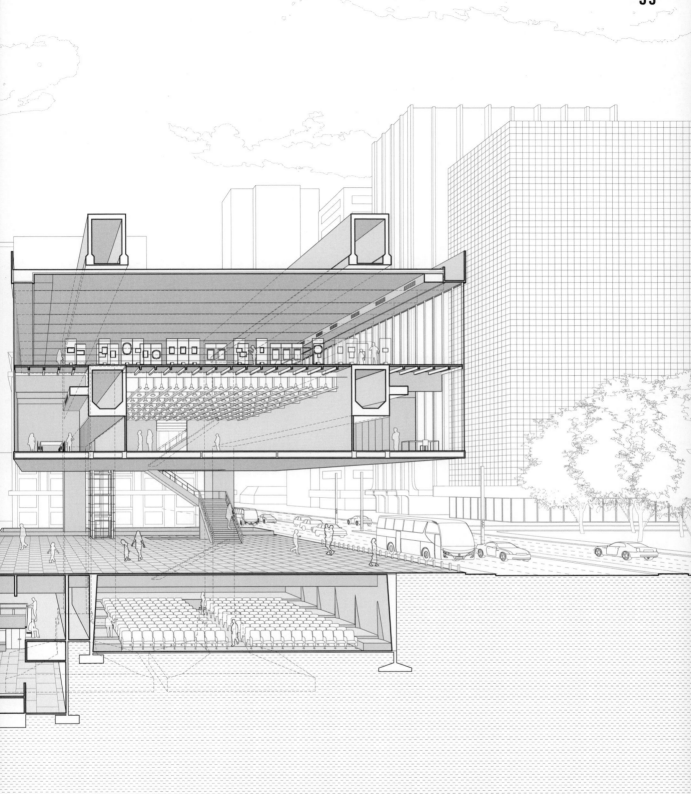

Lina Bo Bardi | 1968

are external, producing an unimpeded exhibition hall enclosed by a curtain wall on all four sides. An external stair and elevator link the suspended volume and the plaza with the below-grade civic hall, auditoriums, theater, library, restaurant, and service spaces. Exploiting the topography of its urban site, this stacked complex is paradoxically both subterranean and floating, camouflaged and monumental, compressed and expansive.

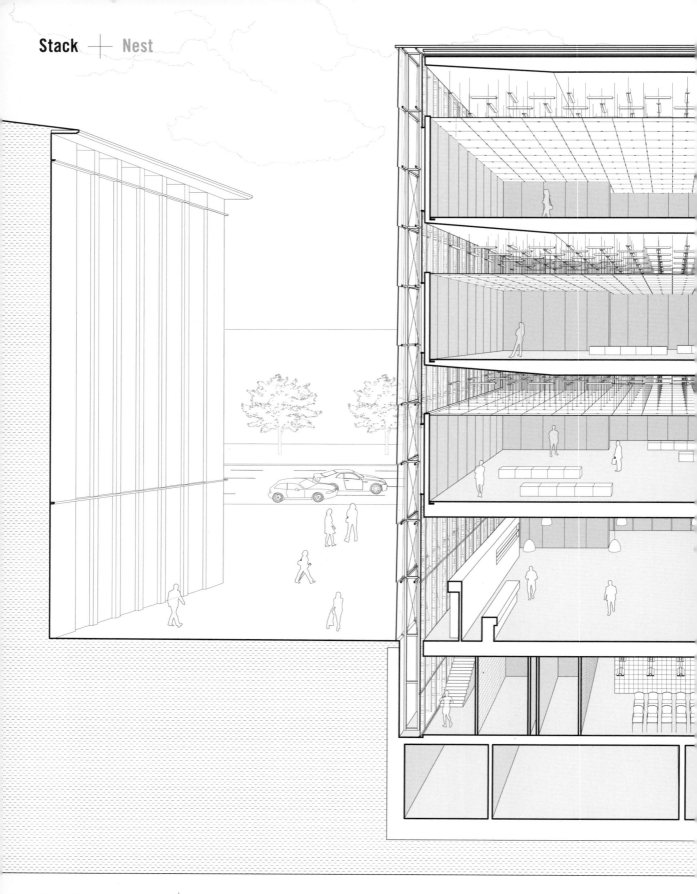

Kunsthaus Bregenz | Bregenz, Austria

This monolithic building's uniform, translucent glass rainscreen veils a complex section. Square in plan, the building is composed of one structure nested inside another. A steel lattice supports both the outer glass shingles and an interior curtain-wall membrane. The 3-ft (91 cm) cavity between the glass layers provides thermal control and light diffusion. Inside, an independent concrete structure positions three exhibition spaces above a ground-floor entry lobby and two subterranean floors that contain an auditorium, an archive, and service spaces. Three walls, offset from

Peter Zumthor | 1997

the perimeter by vertical circulation, support the concrete floors, producing column-free exhibition spaces. Echoing the Salk Institute, a large plenum above each of the exhibit floors allows diffused light from the exterior to illuminate the etched-glass ceiling, augmented by an array of artificial lights in the plenum. Only two of the five publicly accessible floors have the same ceiling height. This project nests a variably extruded stacked section to produce luminous effects on both interior and exterior.

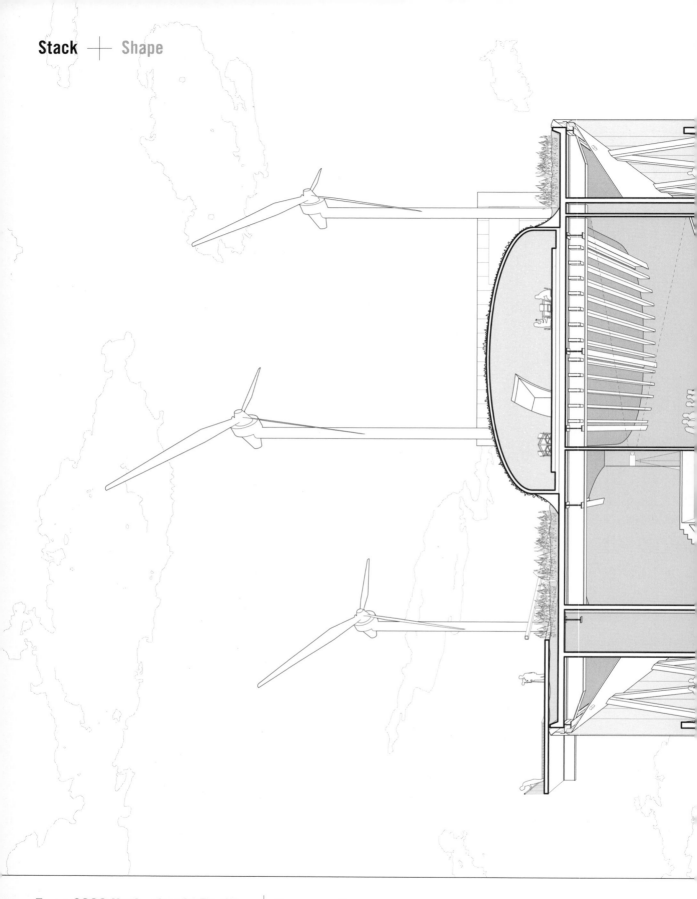

Expo 2000 Netherlands Pavilion | Hanover, Germany

This temporary pavilion placed simulations of six distinct Dutch landscapes directly on top of one another. Moving upward from offices located below grade, visitors encountered dunes, greenhouses, overscaled planters, a forest, and polders. It was a building conceived as a thickness of inhabitable grounds, forming a vertical park with extreme aesthetic, structural, programmatic, and environmental disjunction from floor to floor. Ceiling heights ranged from 8 ft 6 in (2.6 m) to 38 ft 9 in (11.8 m). The structure varied from amorphous concrete bladders to oblique tree trunks to conventional repetitive joists. Each floor was autonomous; there was little direct physical or spatial exchange in section. Egress stairs and elevators were stuck onto the outside of the building and carried all vertical circulation. The uniformity of the circulation structures was in contrast to the variation of the individual floors. Through limited exterior skins, the elevation revealed the sectional nature of the building, rendering the disjunction of floors as the image of the building. Here the stacked section is used not to produce the repetition of a typical plan, but rather to emphasize the differences among levels that retain the same perimeter in plan.

Shaping is a modulation of the flat surface of a section. This adds a particular volume to the section and can occur in a floor or ceiling or both. The ceiling is a more common location for this modulation than the floor, as it does not affect the plan's efficacy. Shaped sections often coordinate large collective programs.

SHAPE

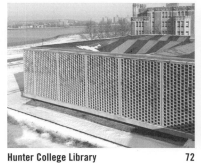

Shape

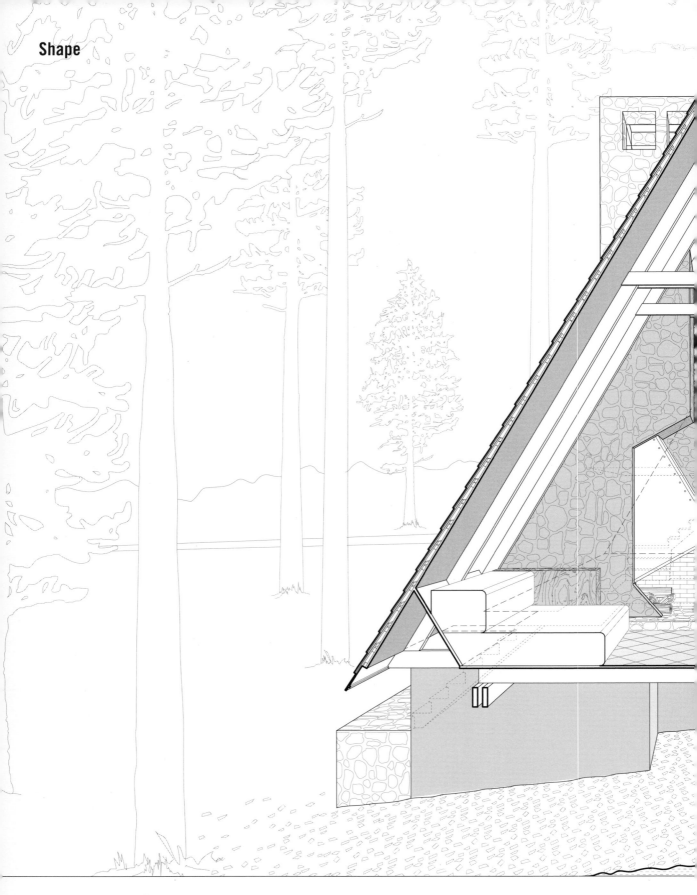

Bennati Cabin | Lake Arrowhead, California, USA

An early example of the A-frame vacation home, this two-bedroom cabin is structured by fourteen equilateral, triangular wood frames, 24 ft (7.3 m) on each side, placed 4 ft (1.2 m) apart. Rather than being positioned above rectilinear walls as in a typical wood-framed house, here the roof reaches down to the bottom of the enclosure. The common spaces of the cabin are on the wider lower level, and two bedrooms with bunks are on the narrower upper level. Pairs of 2-by-8-in (5.1 by 20.3 cm) horizontal beams attached to each 3-by-6-in (7.6 by 15.2 cm) roof rafter support the floors and resist the outward thrust of

Rudolph Schindler | 1937

the roof. Vertical windows, which extend the interior space horizontally, and custom furniture integrated with the acute triangular frame enable the lower corners to be inhabited. The wood building anchors to a stone base that negotiates the topography and extends vertically through the house as the fireplace chimney. A staircase clad in plywood aligns with the chimney. In addition to providing an efficient shape for a wood structure, the section defines the organization of the house and fulfills the mandates of local aesthetic building ordinances, which require Alpine themes.

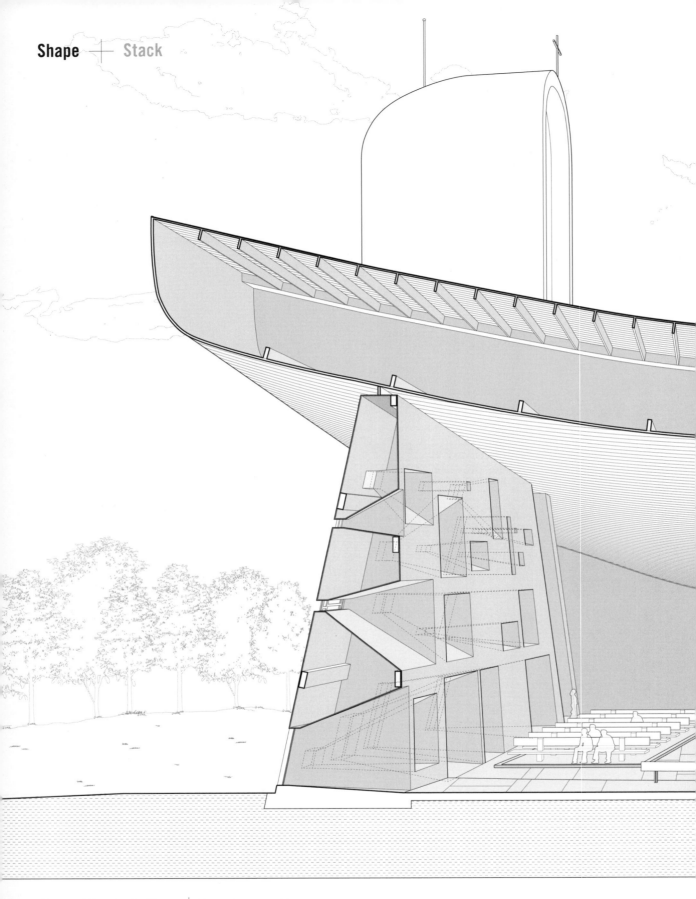

Notre Dame du Haut | Ronchamp, France

The section of Le Corbusier's well-known pilgrimage chapels reveals material and structural paradoxes. Both the south wall and the roof appear to be massive but are hollow. The ceiling, over 7 ft (2.1 m) deep in some areas, is formed by curved concrete girders and parallel purlins that span between the girders. This structural system produces the convex underbelly defining the interior of the church and gathers into a single rain scupper at the rear. The surfaces of the south wall are supported by an internal concrete frame; its pyramidal apertures are formed by thin shells of gunite. In contrast, the other perimeter walls, which appear

Le Corbusier | 1954

less massive than the south wall, are solid—composed of concrete columns and stone salvaged from the chapel that previously occupied the site. The joint between the south wall and the ceiling is mediated by an 8-in (20.3 cm) clerestory of glass, illuminating the curvature of a roof that appears to float unmoored to the south wall.

Following the topography of the site, the floor slopes gently toward the altar. Unlike those religious spaces that use a concave ceiling to gather and focus an interior space, the convex, shaped section of Ronchamp pushes against the periphery, while merging with three smaller chapels at the sides of the nave.

Shape

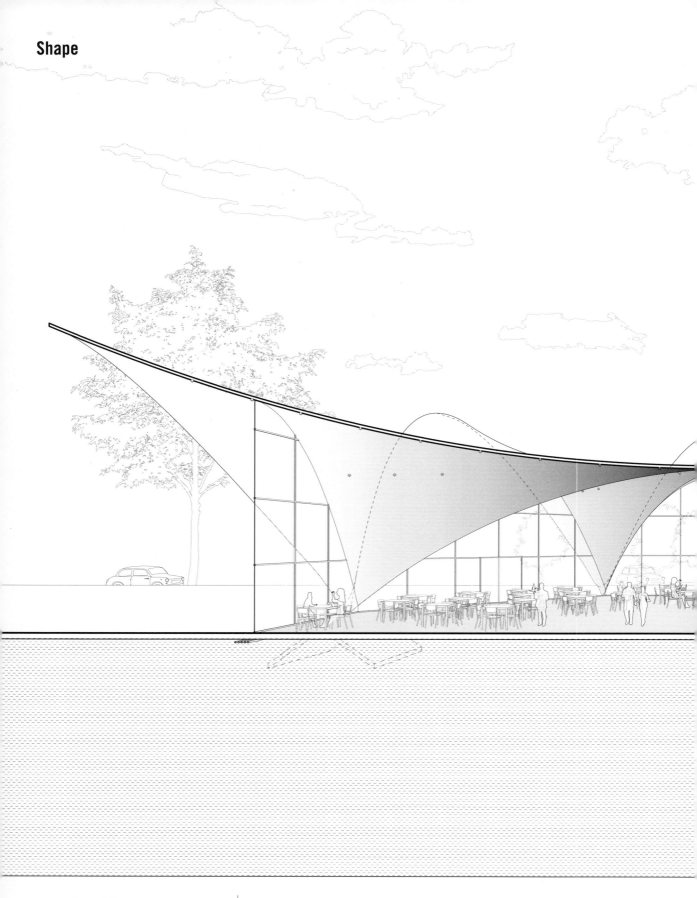

Los Manantiales Restaurant | Mexico City, Mexico

Los Manantiales Restaurant is one of the best-known examples of Félix Candela's thin-shell concrete structures. The building takes the form of four intersecting hyperbolic paraboloids—surfaces that are curved along two planes at once, which can be made by an array of straight wood formwork.

At the valley intersections, V-beams are thickened and reinforced with additional steel, stiffening the base of the groin vaults. The outer edge of the structure reveals the thin 1-5/8-in (4.1 cm) shell, which spans 106 ft (32.3 m) in parabolic saddles at the perimeter of a 139-ft-diameter (42.4 m) space. The shell is

Félix Candela | 1958

19 ft 2 in (5.8 m) high at the middle and 32 ft 7 in (9.9 m) at the tallest outer point and rests on inverted umbrella footings to distribute the load over the site's soft soil. The shape and all of the architecture of this building is determined by its structural form. Although the building is a single space, the roof articulates distinct seating areas at the perimeter of the plan. At the eight bays, curtains of glass enclose the restaurant, provide panoramic views out to the canals and park, and trace hyperbolic curves as they intersect the shell of this shaped section.

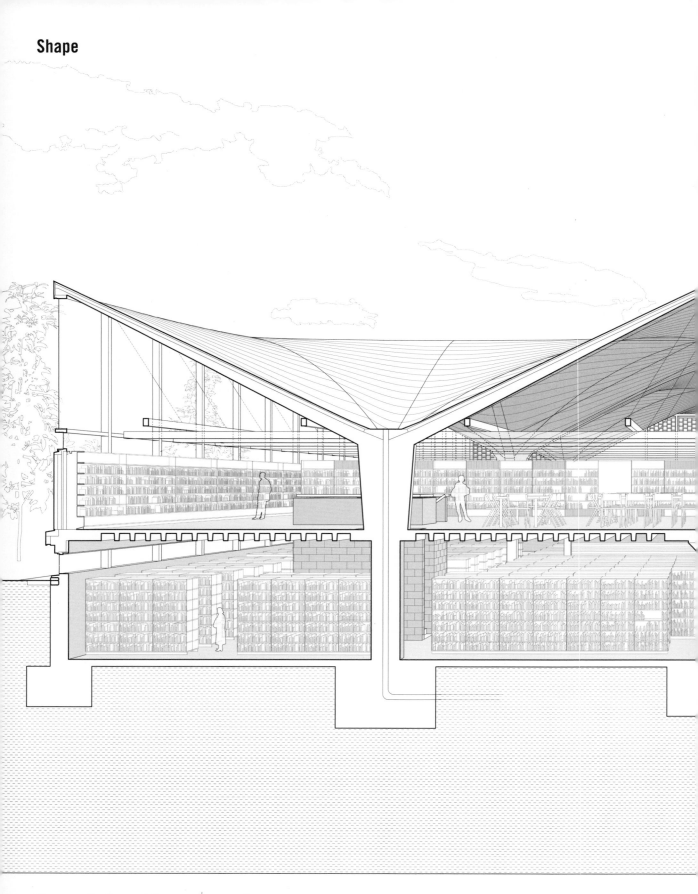

Hunter College Library | New York, New York, USA

This library is one part of a two-building complex, with the other building housing administrative offices and classrooms. The library contains a 120-by-180-ft (36.6 by 54.9 m) reading room on its upper floor and bookstacks, offices, and support spaces in a mostly underground lower floor. The rectangular plan is spanned by six inverted umbrellas placed 60 ft (18.3 m) apart on center, extending 35 ft 5 in (10.8 m) from the lowest level to the top of the roof. These calyxes are tied together to provide lateral bracing, support the perimeter glass walls, and define the volume of the reading room. In addition, water collects in the calyxes and flows

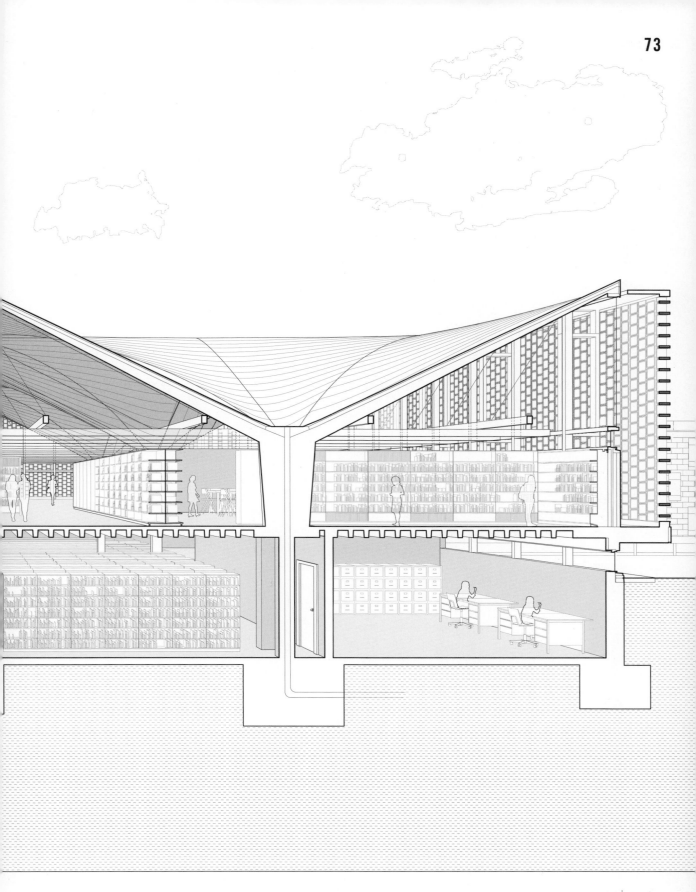

Marcel Breuer | 1960

through drains internal to the cruciform columns. The umbrellas take the shape of a hyperbolic paraboloid, composed of a thin concrete shell shaped by the formwork's straight lines of stock lumber. A suspended aluminum ceiling grid supports a field of linear lights, which are a counterpoint to the curves of the ceiling above. The east and south walls are lined with an external sunscreen formed from terra-cotta flue tiles. In this shaped section the building's topographic ceiling follows directly from the geometry of its structural shell, animating a rectilinear plan with an undulating volume of space.

Shape

Seinäjoki Library | Seinäjoki, Finland

This library forms one side of a municipal campus center. Its plan is composed of a rectangular bar of classrooms and support spaces merged with a fan-shaped volume for bookstacks and reading areas. Located at the intersection of the bar and the fan is the circulation desk. The cast-in-place concrete ceiling and floor are both adjusted in section to modulate light and to facilitate views within the interior. Above the outer perimeter of the fan of books, the concave ceiling diffuses southern light into the library, while a gently sloped ceiling distributes northern light from a clerestory above the central desk.

Alvar Aalto | 1965

A sunken reading area, typical of Aalto's libraries, provides a sequestered environment in the center of the stacks. This subdued experience is reinforced by the darker middle section of the ceiling, whose concave surface receives limited light. This sunken area is positioned to remain visible from the circulation desk. The shape of the interior is not visible on the exterior, due to a large roof cavity that contains upturned beams, which support the undulating ceiling. In this shaped section the floor and the ceiling are modulated in tandem to enhance the spatial qualities and performance of the program.

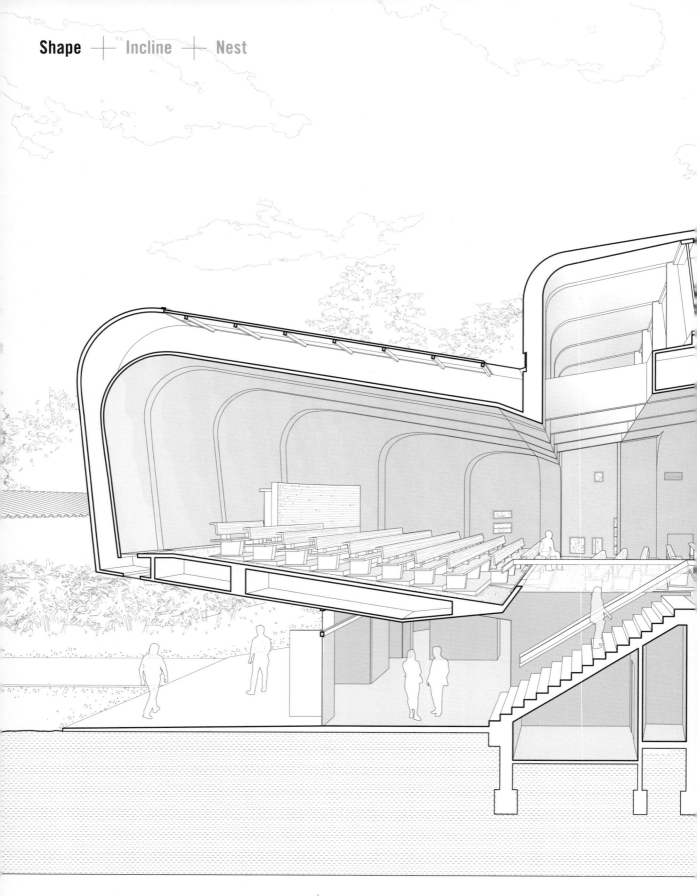

Church of Sainte-Bernadette du Banlay | Nevers, France

This small church contains a grottolike nave above a ground floor of classrooms and support rooms. What appears from the outside to be a cast-
in-place, board-formed concrete monolith is revealed in the section to be
composed of two thin shells of concrete wrapped around thirteen parallel

structural frames. This suspended sanctuary, the outer edges of which
cantilever beyond the central structural plinth, is accessed from a stair that
emerges at the center of the space. With a floor deflecting both down and
up toward the altar, this is one of the few built examples of Claude Parent

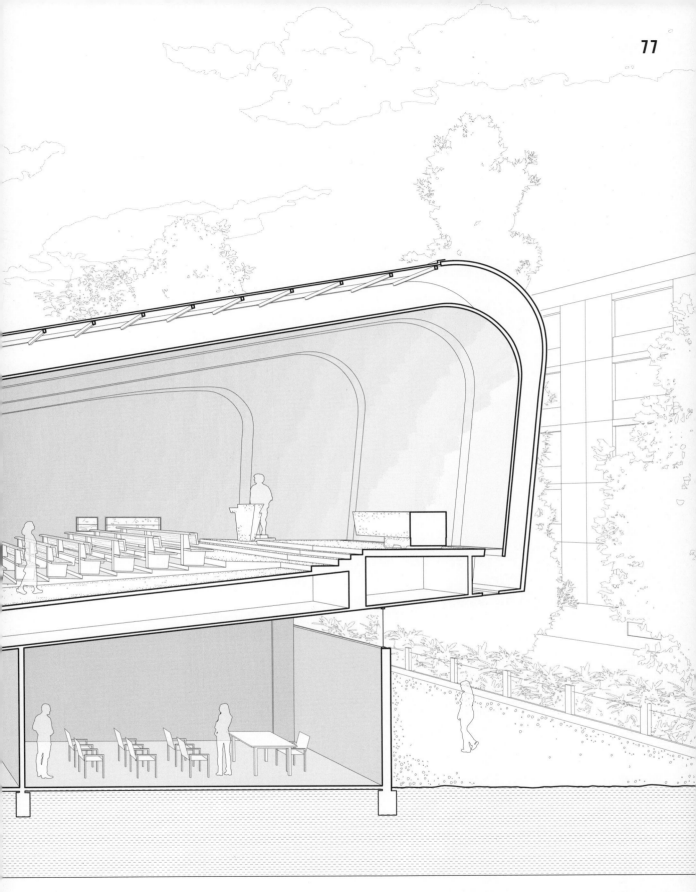

Claude Parent and Paul Virilio | 1966

and Paul Virilio's *la fonction oblique*, a critique of the modern plan intended to provoke future social organizations predicated on inclined surfaces. Heavily influenced by Virilio's archaeological work on World War II bunkers, the church is the intersection of two convex inclined volumes, offset in plan, whose joint is marked by a central skylight that extends across the full width of the nave. The central location of natural light, the direct entry into the congregation from below, and the inflected floor all upend conventions of the sectional organization of Western churches.

Shape

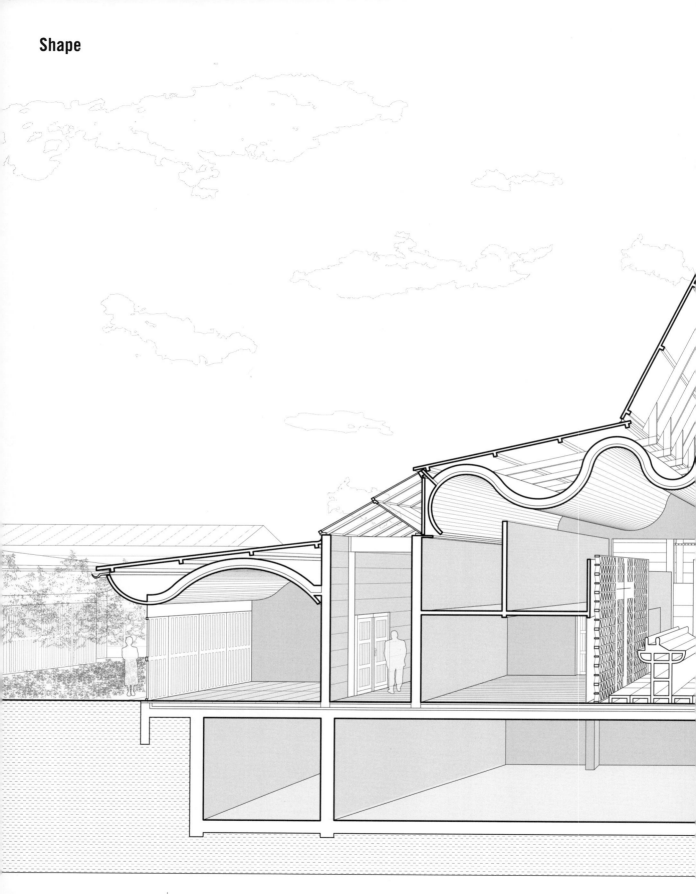

Bagsværd Church | Copenhagen, Denmark

In plan, the chapel of the Church at Bagsværd is the central space in a rectangular collection of rooms and courtyards, which are framed by perimeter aisles used for circulation throughout the church. Natural light enters primarily through a large skylight located between the two uppermost folds of the curved ceiling, as well as through the glass ceilings of the perimeter aisles. The surface of this ceiling, which is at its lowest above the entry, compressing space over the congregation, vaults skyward toward the altar and accentuates lines of sight beyond the sacristy. A sequence of

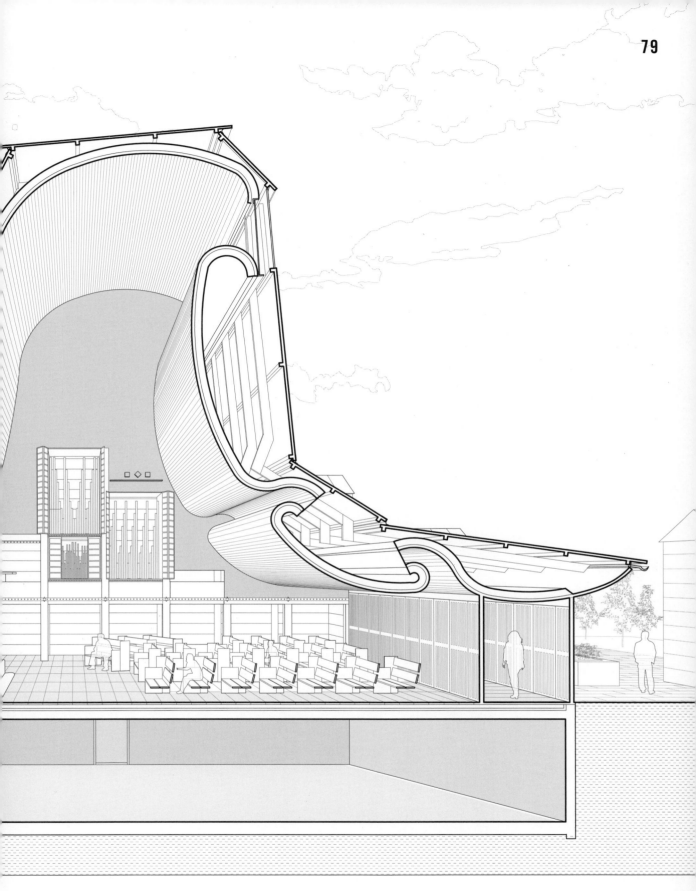

Jørn Utzon | 1976

connected arcs evoking layers of clouds forms the sectional geometry of the ceiling. The ceiling is composed of thin board-formed concrete shells, which span 63 ft 8 in (19.4 m) between the two perimeter aisles and support the external metal roof. The structural relationship between the

ceiling and roof inverts the typical hierarchy, in which interior surfaces are supported by exterior structure. In this shaped section, the voluminous quality of the interior stands in extreme contrast to the flat surfaces of the exterior massing.

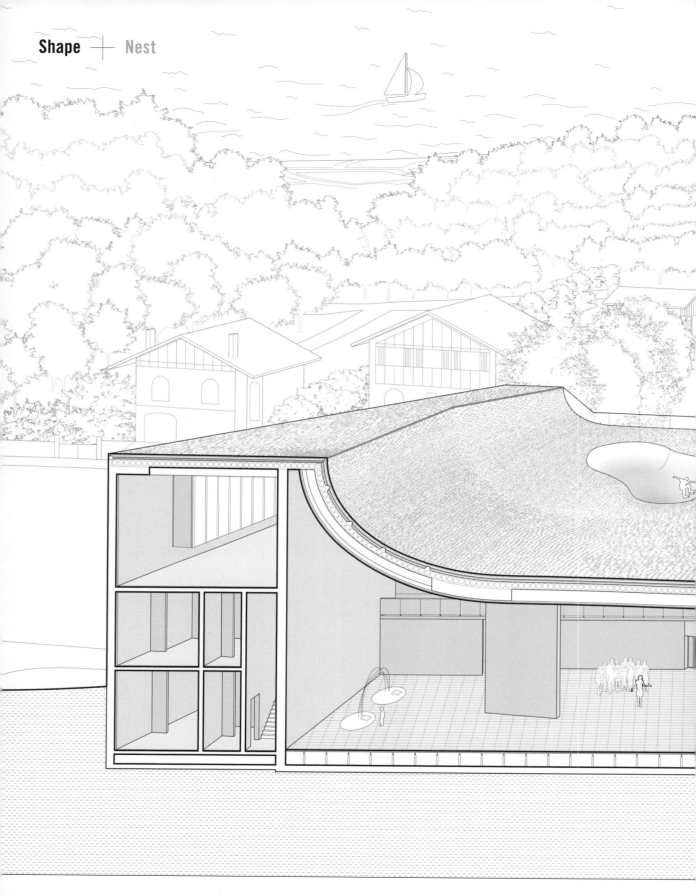

Cité de l'Océan et du Surf │ Biarritz, France

This museum adjacent to the beaches of Biarritz, France, takes both its subject matter and architectural approach from the surrounding landscape. A concave surface of 31-1/2-in-thick (80 cm), hollow-core structural concrete curves up out of the site's topography to define a rooftop public plaza while simultaneously shaping the ceiling of the museum below. The exterior plaza is covered in cobblestones and grass and is animated by a skate "pool" and two large, glazed volumes housing a restaurant and a kiosk for surfers. Slipping below the raised edges of the plaza, visitors enter a large, double-height exhibition space edged by service areas, offices, and an

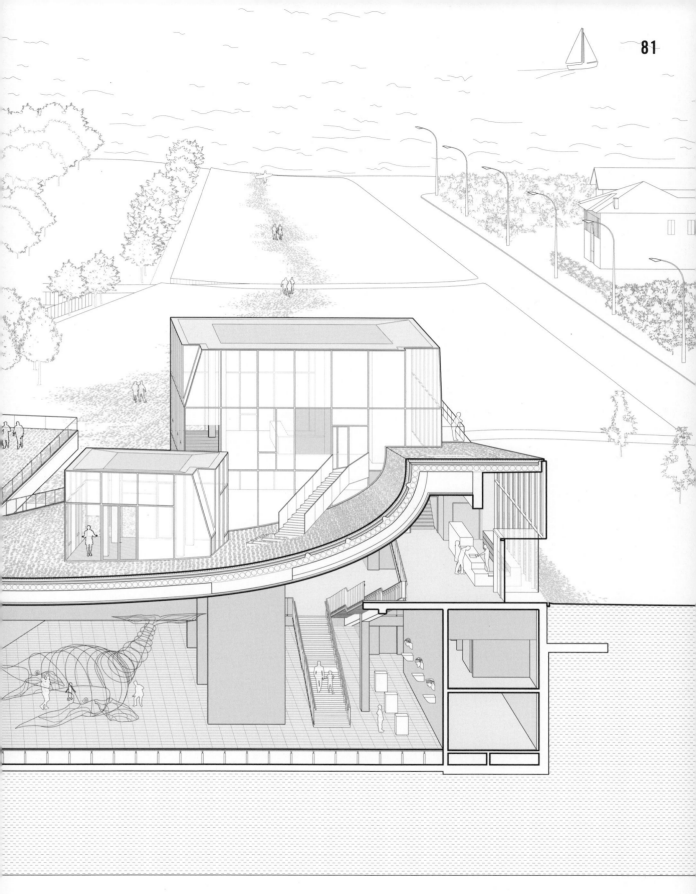

auditorium. The single shaped and inclined surface of the roof creates two contrasting spaces: one above, one below; one exterior, one interior; one expansive and open to the sky, the other sheltered beneath the convex swell of the massive roof. The building's exterior expression exhibits its own dualities of form: on the side farthest from the ocean, the curving section of the plaza produces a defined edge, while the seaward side blends seamlessly into the surrounding terrain as an inclined surface. The cobblestone and grass materiality of the plaza extends the dynamic space of this hybrid section toward the water as a public path and garden.

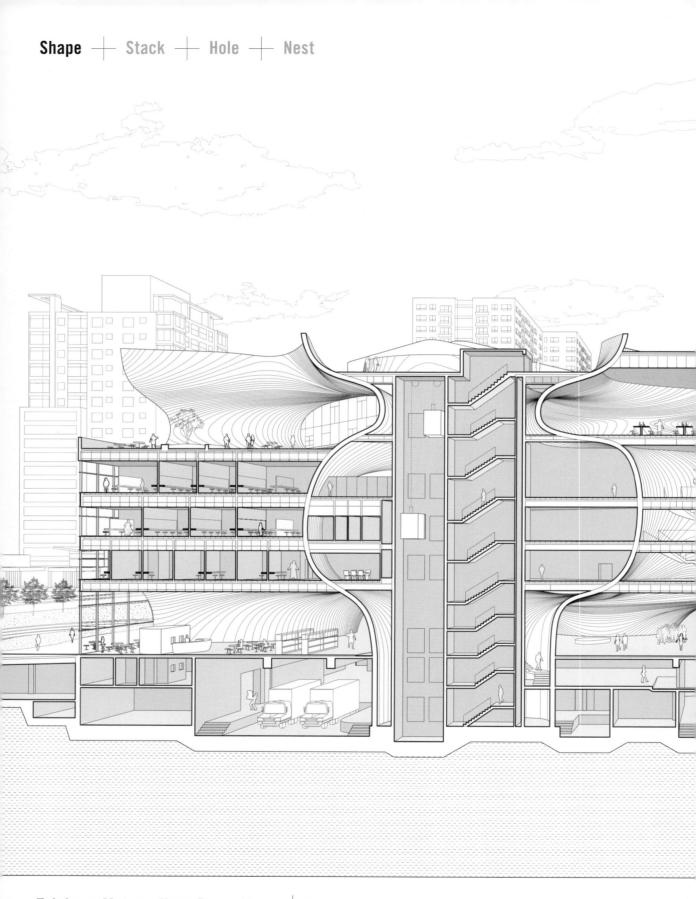

Taichung Metropolitan Opera House | Taichung, Taiwan

This opera house, containing a two-thousand-seat grand theater, an eight-hundred-seat playhouse, and a two-hundred-seat black box theater, is articulated by a continuous topological grid, using three-dimensional curved forms to eradicate distinctions between horizontal and vertical surfaces.

Formed from fifty-eight catenoids and built by spraying concrete onto a sequence of steel truss walls that rationalize the complex form, the primary space-defining structure is horizontal only at brief points of tangency. Programs are held on stacked horizontal floors that are nested within the

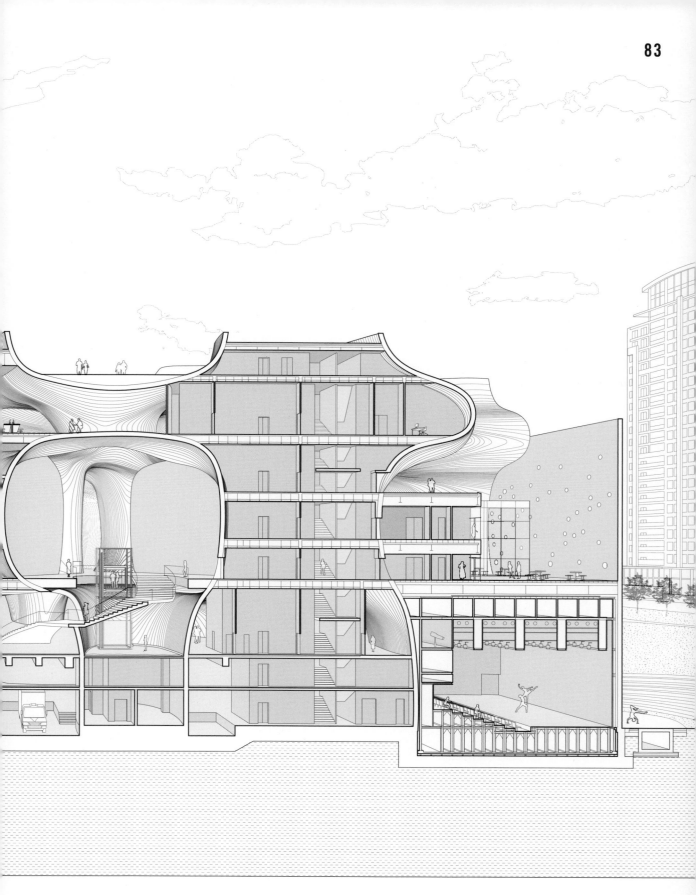

Toyo Ito & Associates | 2016

curved surfaces. The shaped sections of these curved surfaces are therefore visible as walls and ceilings or as the perimeter of circulation spaces and atrium voids, but rarely as floors. The facades are rendered as cuts through the building diagram. The roughly 1-ft-thick (30.5 cm) structural curves of this hybrid section are infilled with curtain wall or porous shotcrete, or left open to render the inflected spaces as exterior voids.

Shear induces a rift or cut parallel to either the horizontal or vertical axis of section. This type of section is particularly effective at inducing optical, thermal, or acoustic connections within an extruded or stacked section without significantly compromising the tectonic efficiencies of repetition upon which those types are based.

SHEAR

Shear — Hole

13 Rue des Amiraux | Paris, France

Filling three sides of a city block, this social housing project comprises seventy-eight apartments on seven floors above two floors for collective programs or utility spaces. Henri Sauvage's use of the horizontal shear was innovative at the time. Each floor steps back 3 ft 3 in (1 m), creating enhanced exterior terraces and guaranteeing exposure to the sky for the apartments. Each apartment has either three or four rooms; in both cases, all rooms are placed along the building's perimeter. Supported by a concrete structure clad in ceramic tile, the pyramid-shaped building allows light and air into both the apartments and the

Henri Sauvage | 1930

surrounding streets. A swimming pool lined with changing rooms is in the center of the sheared section and is supported by a series of mechanical rooms for heat and ventilation below. Small storage rooms for the apartments are located adjacent to the central skylight for the pool. This building has served as the model for numerous subsequent variations on the horizontally sheared section. In this type, dwellings or other individualized units are often located on the upper side of a rake facing the sky, while a collective social program not requiring natural light often occupies the void between the rake and the ground.

Shear

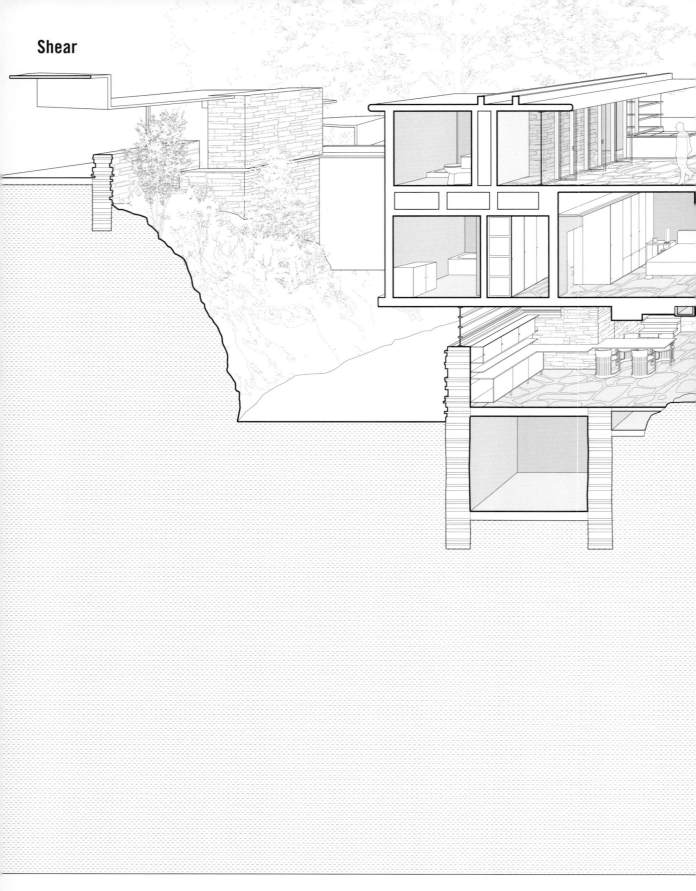

Fallingwater | Mill Run, Pennsylvania, USA

Frank Lloyd Wright's famous vacation house in rural Pennsylvania is accessed by a drive that crosses a small bridge and wraps around the building, distinguishing the house from the hillside. Inside, the building consists of a main open-plan living room floor and two floors for bedrooms above. Concrete piers cast into the existing rocks form the building's foundation. The house is anchored to this foundation by load-bearing walls clad in local stone. Concrete waffle-slab floors cantilever as far as eighteen feet over the stream. A large site boulder emerges through the floor as the

Frank Lloyd Wright | 1939

hearth in the living room. Ceiling heights vary within and across rooms, some as low as 6-ft-4-in (1.9 m). Unlike more typical uses of horizontal shear, the cantilevered trays do not replicate each other in plan, but rather project in three different directions and have different lengths and widths.

These variations produce a calculated array of overhangs and terraces on all sides of the house. In this sheared section, the cantilevers visually, acoustically, and formally extend and embed the substance of the house in the landscape, while simultaneously echoing the stacked rocks of the site.

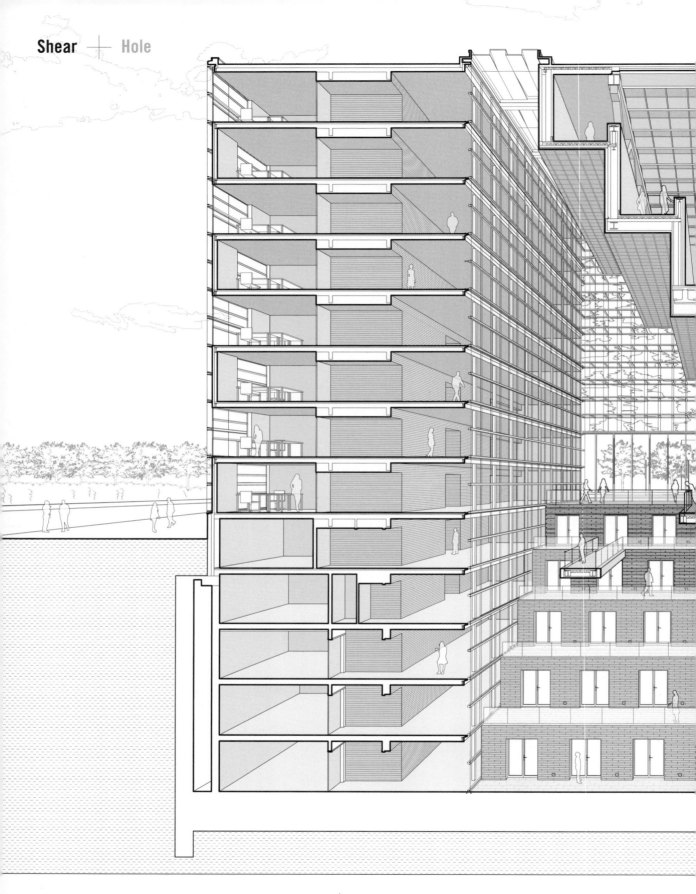

Shear + Hole

Netherlands Institute for Sound and Vision | Hilversum, the Netherlands

This rectilinear volume contains a research institute and national archives for Dutch television and radio. Limited to a height of 82 ft (25 m) above ground, the building is divided into a thirteen-story block of offices and technical installations, five stories of archives below grade, and three floors of

exhibition space floating above a large central hall. Light travels from the skylight and the stained-glass facades down through the atrium into the slate-clad archive. Entered at grade, the space of the central hall extends both down into a stepped canyon crossed by three bridges and

Neutelings Riedijk Architects | 2006

up into a ziggurat-shaped void adjacent to the exhibition floors. The descending and ascending spaces shear in perpendicular directions, torquing the internal space. This sheared section is less notable for its impact on the interiors within the sheared floors than for its shaping of the atrium. Carved into the center of the building, the atrium paradoxically emphasizes the programmatic division among three volumes while joining the assembly of this sheared section into a legible whole.

The Mountain Dwellings | Copenhagen, Denmark

The Mountain Dwellings comprises a zone of apartments above a parking garage. The apartments are accessed from the parking garage side, through an inclined elevator that connects the parking levels to residential corridors on each level. Each apartment is configured around its own large, L-shaped courtyard, which is lined by built-in planters, providing some visual separation among apartments. The north and west facades are covered in aluminum panels, perforated for ventilation in the image of Mount Everest. Indebted to a long history of buildings that place parking in the underbelly of a horizontally sheared

BIG-Bjarke Ingels Group / JDS Architects | 2008

section of housing, this project has an extreme rake of 25 degrees that accommodates 480 parking spaces—far more than the number needed for its 80 apartments (the building was intended initially as a parking structure). This horizontal shear also produces a high degree of exposure to the sky, which is capitalized on by the courtyards.

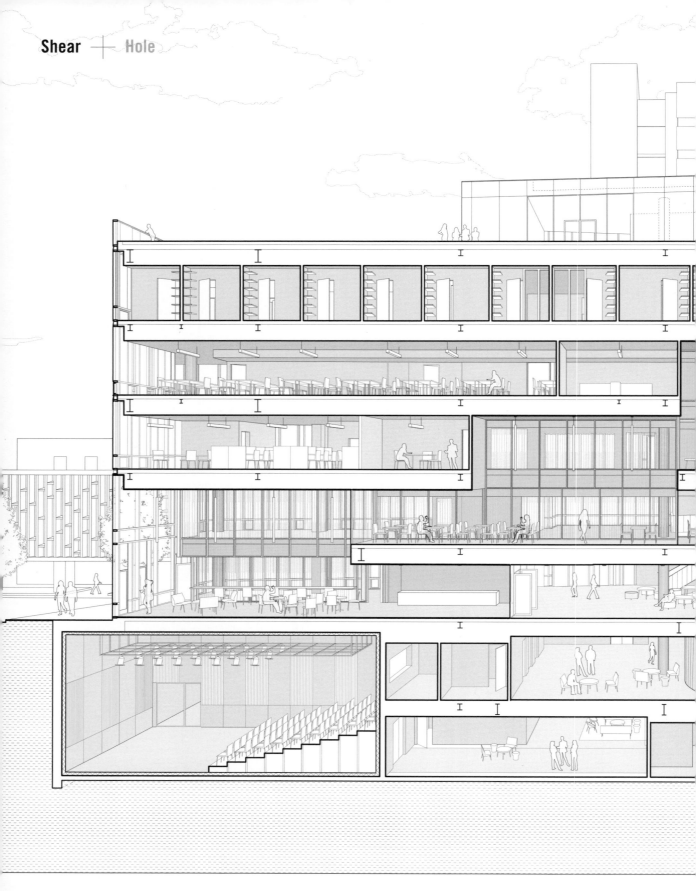

Barnard College Diana Center | New York, New York, USA

Situated parallel to Broadway, this arts center encompasses studios, class-rooms, offices, exhibition galleries, a black-box theater, a cafe, a dining room, and a five-hundred-seat circular performance space. Four double-height spaces are stacked diagonally, producing a visually continuous void

through the center of the building. This void is registered on the east facade (facing Broadway) through the articulation of custom-fritted glass panels. Separated by clear glass for acoustic reasons and fire mitigation, these volumes each contain a distinct social program and collectively allow

Weiss/Manfredi | 2010

visual links throughout the building as well as to the adjacent campus lawn. Academic programs are distributed around the oblique void, with the largest space—a circular performance hall—located under the horizontal shear. On the side facing west, circulation extends into glass volumes that cantilever outside the building's footprint. This section combines the spatial and optical effects of a hole section with the cumulative consequence of a horizontal shear.

Apollo Schools—Willemspark School | Amsterdam, the Netherlands

The Apollo Schools comprises two buildings designed as complementary elementary schools. This section is taken through the Willemspark School, looking east toward the Montessori School. Both schools are organized by the same spatial diagram, in which a central space rises through a stepped, sheared section, connecting to classrooms in each of the four corners. Where the shear is not mediated by stairs, larger steps form seats, making the shear a gathering point. This section replaces the typical school's generic classroom corridor with an animated auditorium at the heart of the

Herman Hertzberger | 1983

school, used for impromptu performances and organized daily activities. Rounded skylights illuminate the central space, balancing the solidity of walls designed to focus the learning environment inward. While allowing views between floors, this sheared section simultaneously preserves privacy within each of the classrooms by preventing diagonal views from entering the heart of the teaching spaces.

Shear

Granoff Center for the Creative Arts | Providence, Rhode Island, USA

Defined by an emphatic vertical shear, this creative arts center combines a recital hall, electrical shop, recording studio, and production studios on its south side with a gallery, wood shop, multimedia room, and an additional production studio on the north side. A ground-level circulation corridor, wide enough to be a lounge, is lodged between the recital hall and gallery, enabling views into multiple floors of the building. Mechanical systems at the ceiling are mostly exposed, and cast-in-place concrete floors span east to west, parallel to a 10-in-wide (25.4 cm) double-glazed

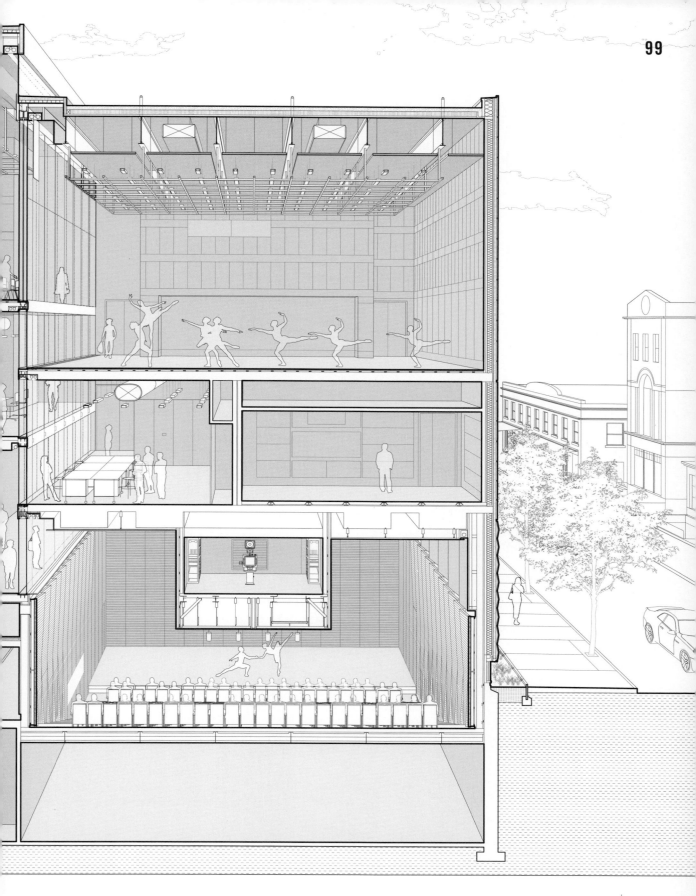

Diller Scofidio + Renfro | 2011

dividing wall, allowing the glass to be free of dropped ceilings and columns. This glass wall maintains acoustic separations among the programs while intensifying optical exchanges in order to foster interdisciplinarity. Retractable blinds are located between the panes of glass to control light and privacy. Recognizing that a vertical shear creates circulatory discontinuity, the design locates a large staircase at the rear of the building to gather the multiple levels of the section into a collective area, complete with landings that double as lounges.

Holes are a pragmatic and frequently used means to produce a section, and range in scale and quantity from a single small opening between two floors to multiple large atria organizing whole buildings. Holes exchange lost floor area for benefits in section. They are a spatial commodity that can be tactically deployed for vertical effects.

HOLE

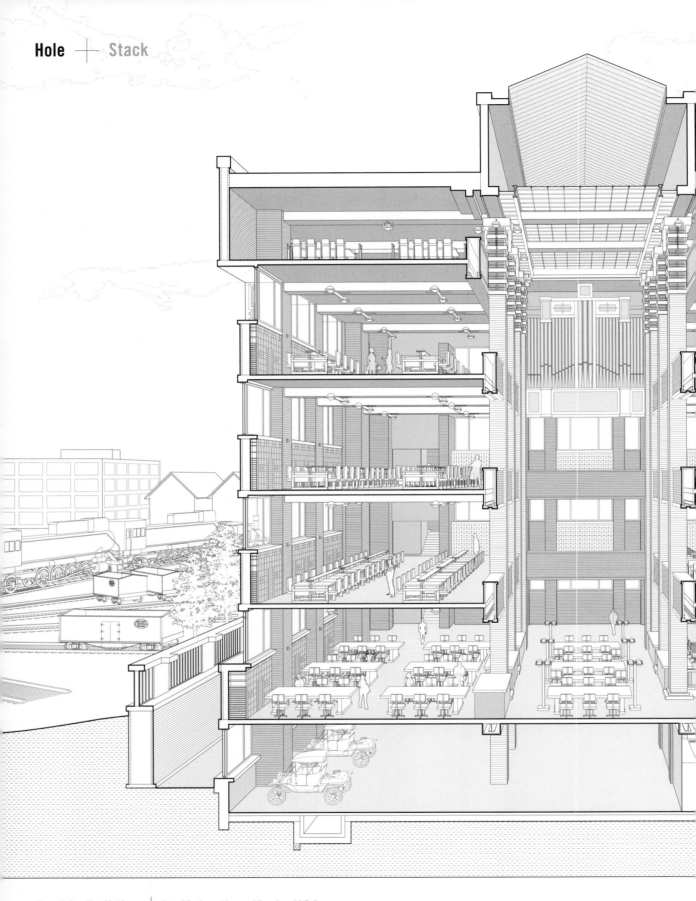

Larkin Building | Buffalo, New York, USA

This headquarters for a soap company contained four prominent floors of open desks; a basement for parking and file storage; and a restaurant, kitchen, and conservatory on its uppermost level. Accessed from the east side of the building (seen on the right side of the drawing), the central atrium was 25 ft 3 in (7.7 m) wide, 112 ft (34.1 m) long, and 76 ft 0 in (23.2 m) high. A double-skin glass skylight capped the atrium, allowing the high-ceilinged (16 ft [4.9 m] floor to floor) open-plan office floors to be naturally illuminated. The building was steel framed with reinforced-concrete floors. The perimeter of each office floor was lined with

Frank Lloyd Wright | 1906

filing cabinets at the base and a double-layer glass clerestory above eye level. The filing cabinets restricted visual access to the outside, redirecting views toward the interior atrium. Air-conditioning was distributed in the hollow guardrails ringing the atrium, cooling a hermetically sealed environment that protected employees from the pollution of the surrounding industrial landscape. Staircases integrated with vertical chases, drawing air into the mechanical system, were located at the four corners of the building. The scale of the atrium balanced optical and thermal performance, and its openness encouraged a sense of collective effort.

Single House at Weissenhofsiedlung | Stuttgart, Germany

Le Corbusier's single-family home for a middle-class family, exhibited at the 1927 Weissenhof housing exhibition, serves as an early realization of the Citrohan box, a prototype living unit organized around a double-height hole in the center of the section. Embodying the structure of Le Corbusier's "five points of a new architecture," the house rests on two rows of five concrete columns, each spaced 8 ft 2 in (2.5 m) apart. The columns are exposed as *pilotis* at ground level. On the upper floors one row of columns is encased in the exterior wall; the other frames one side of the staircase. The third-floor plate is cut back

Le Corbusier | 1927

diagonally, forming an angled balcony that allows the parents' bedroom, bath, and boudoir on the mezzanine to overlook the double-height living room below. A two-story glass wall made of two independent layers of operable windows creates a thermal double skin and interstitial greenhouse. The top floor is split into an open-air terrace, complete with a nonglazed ribbon window, and a nested combination of bedrooms. The dividing partition between the bedrooms serves as a storage closet for beds and linens. In this prototypical house for the machine age, a hole section is used to organize modern domestic life.

Hole ┼ Stack ┼ Shear

Ford Foundation Headquarters | New York, New York, USA

Featuring an interior garden, the glazed atrium at the heart of the Ford Foundation Headquarters strikes a balance between individual privacy and collective enterprise. Because the program required substantially less space than the permitted buildable volume, the Ford Foundation turned excess space into a civic amenity. The 179-ft-high (54.6 m) atrium, asymmetrically located in the southeast corner of the building, visually interconnects the offices while providing views diagonally to the East River. Steel beams spanning 84 ft (25.6 m) hold the ten-story glass facades on the south and east sides,

Kevin Roche John Dinkeloo and Associates | 1968

which open the garden to public view and fill the interior courtyard with light. Banks
of offices with fully glazed windows that allow the temperate greenhouse air to circulate
overlook the atrium on its north and west side. The executive suite, a collective dining
facility, and an expansive skylight cap the top of this holed section.

Hole + Stack

Phillips Exeter Academy Library | Exeter, New Hampshire, USA

At the heart of the Exeter library is a 70-ft-high (21.3 m) atrium framed on all four sides by concrete structure. Capped by a monumental 16-ft-deep (4.9 m) concrete brace-frame and wrapped in a timber-clad clerestory, this central hole or atrium draws light into the middle of the 111-by-111-ft (33.8 by 33.8 m) square library, illuminating the circulation and reference floor below. Multistory circular holes on each side of the atrium reveal the wood-clad balconies of each floor and the stacks behind the balconies, which extend to the outer edges of the building. At the periphery, 210

Louis I. Kahn | 1972

built-in private carrels merge wooden furniture with the exterior brick skin, creating a synthetic wall section in which materials indicate use. The profile of the concrete floor slab integrates lighting fixtures, mechanical systems, balconies, and staircases while accommodating the sizable structural load of the collection. While this holed section animates a twentieth-century library, brick piers produce a crenellated effect along the perimeter ambulatory, echoing the medieval legacy of libraries.

Hole ┼ Stack ┼ Shear

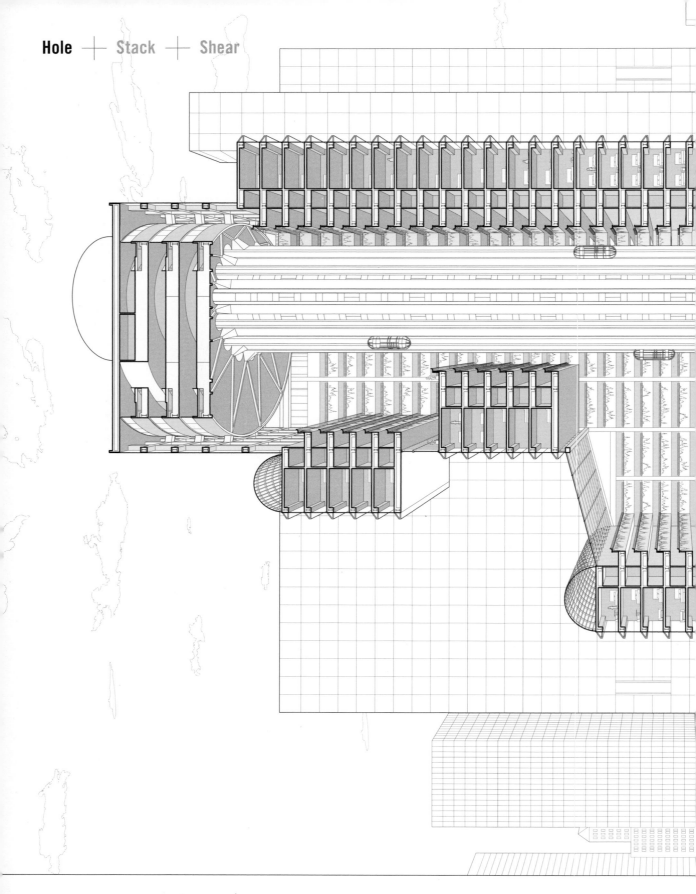

New York Marriott Marquis | New York, New York, USA

The Marriott Marquis is one of many hotels designed by John Portman that are organized around an excessively large interior atrium. The building is primarily structured by two vertical bars on the north and south sides, which are composed of a steel frame and precast-concrete planks. A third vertical bar on the west connects the parallel bars, and a series of five-floor stacks span the east facade, which faces Times Square. The 470-ft (143.3 m) atrium is wrapped by 1,876 hotel rooms. Repetitive bands formed by open corridors and hanging plants intensify the vertiginous effect of the atrium. In the five cascading volumes facing Times Square,

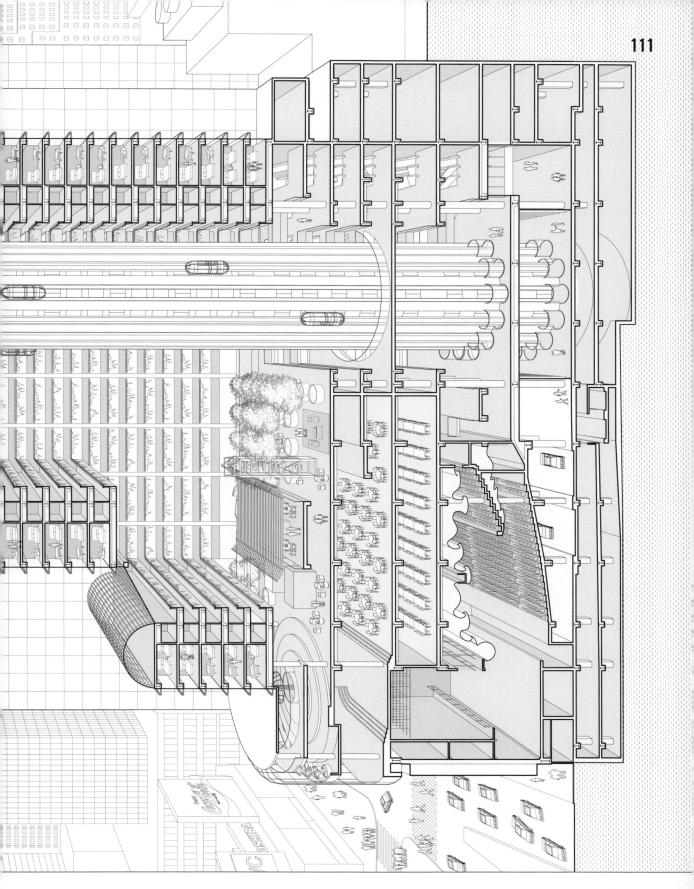

John Portman & Associates | 1985

lounges provide views to the street and atrium below. Twelve glass elevators ascend the atrium along a central concrete shaft, linking three floors of revolving restaurants and lounges at the top of the building to the thick plinth below, which contains ballrooms, a 1,500-seat Broadway theater, and many meeting rooms. At the hotel's entrance an internal street feeds to a bank of escalators that rise eight floors to the 30,000-sq-ft (2,787 sq m) sky lobby at the base of the atrium. In this holed section, the merits of Portman's spectacular interior are qualified by the internal environment's disengagement from Times Square.

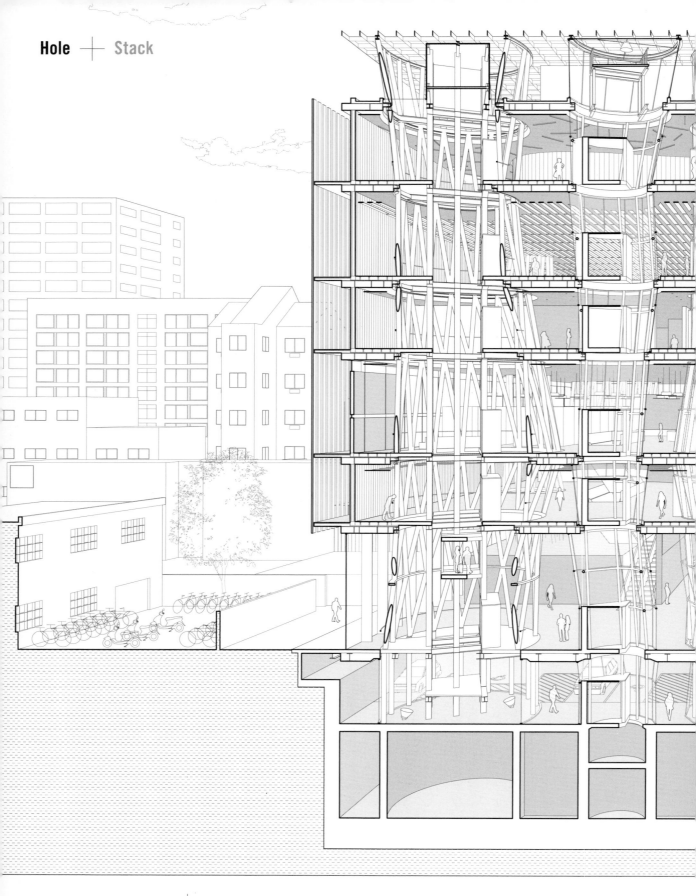

Hole ┼ Stack

Sendai Mediatheque │ Sendai, Japan

In the Sendai Mediatheque structural columns puncture the floors, producing holes for the section. Thirteen vertical, steel-lattice tubes provide
circulation of air, water, electricity, light, and people throughout eight levels
of the building. Built and assembled in floor-height segments, the tubes

are joined by steel rings embedded in each floor slab. The structure of the
floor plates, which are 15 3/4 in (40 cm) thick and resemble a honeycomb
pattern in plan, allows each floor to span between the irregularly spaced
tubes that paradoxically cut holes into the floors they support. While

Toyo Ito & Associates | 2000

structurally robust, the light lattice structure of the tubes maintains sight lines both within individual floors and down through the stacked floor plates. The tubes are clad in glass to mitigate the spread of smoke and fire. Each floor serves a semiautonomous function, containing public meeting spaces, a library, galleries, studios, cinemas, and offices, but the floors are united by the holed section that in turn provides the iconic image of the building.

41 Cooper Square | New York, New York, USA

This academic and laboratory building for Cooper Union comprises a rectilinear stack animated by a complex, figural sectional void. While the majority of the building is composed of a conventional structural-steel grid, canted concrete piers at ground level facilitate a fluid relationship with the street and allow

visual access to public gallery and auditorium spaces below grade. Above, a central atrium carves into the stacked floors of laboratories, offices, and classrooms rising the full height of the building. This torquing atrium creates visual, social, and circulational exchanges among floors while introducing daylight and augmenting

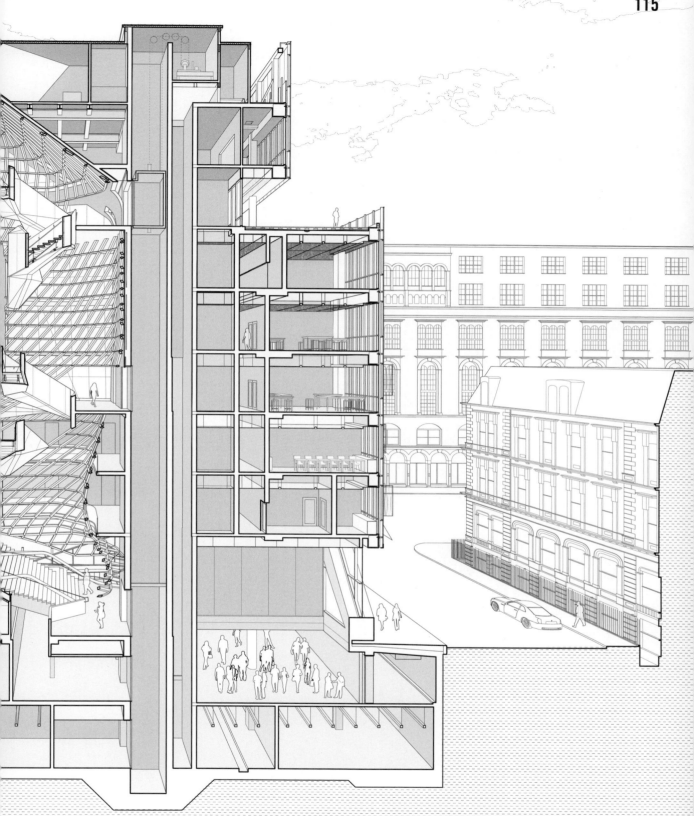

air flow. Defined by a twisting lattice of steel pipes encased in glass-fiber reinforced gypsum, the atrium is at once a hole and a nested figure, containing within its upper levels sculptural stairs clad in translucent, back-lit panels. A monumental stair links the entry to a double-height student lounge at the fourth floor that provides views of the city. This stair serves as a site of both movement and gathering. It combines a shaped ceiling and floor and functions as a distortion and extension of the atrium. The figure of the atrium intersects with the perforated stainless-steel panels of the west facade, linking the building to its urban context.

Inclines are a means of continuing a horizontal surface in section by changing the angle of an occupiable horizontal plane, thus rotating the plane into section. Unlike Stacks, Shears and Holes, Inclines are not based on the distinction between plan and section. With Inclines, section does not require the sacrifice of a portion of the plan.

INCLINE

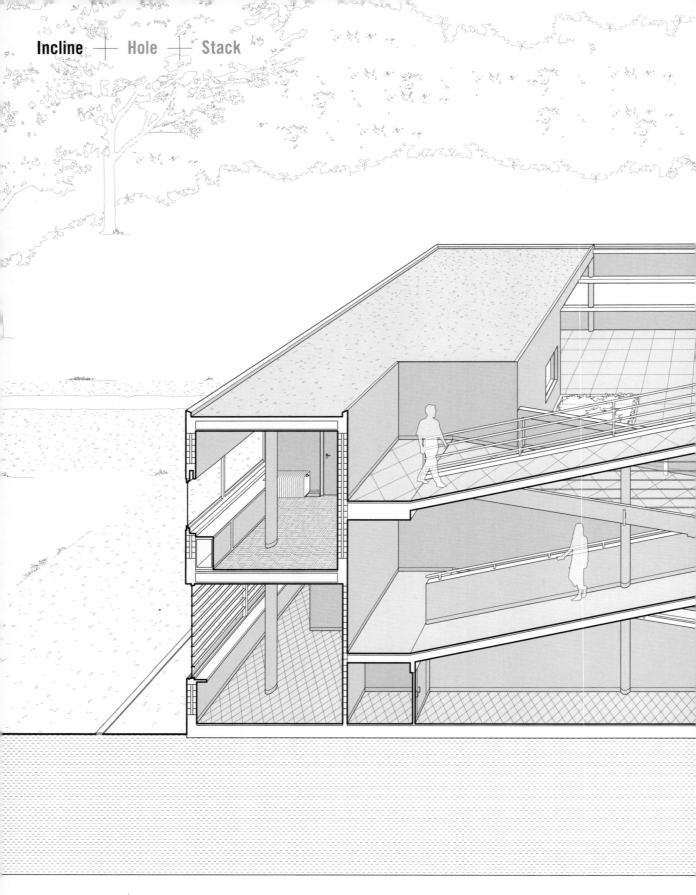

Villa Savoye | Poissy, France

The ramp at the center of Le Corbusier's Villa Savoye orchestrates circulation through the villa and holds a seminal position in the history of architecture as the quintessential example of *promenade architecturale*. Located on axis with the front door, this central ramp provides a continuous walkable surface linking the ground floor to the exterior courtyard terrace of the piano nobile and rooftop solarium. Yet sectional continuity comes with discontinuity of plan. The 4-ft-1-in-wide (1.25 m) ramp produces 32 ft of plan discontinuity on each side. The ramp disrupts the regular column grid and

Le Corbusier | 1931

creates a vertical cut at the heart of the villa, dividing inside from outside. Vertical glass infill between the sloped ramp planes draws daylight onto the ramp and illuminates the center of the rectangular villa. The solid, cast-in-place concrete of the ramps is juxtaposed with the ceramic infill of the concrete floor slabs, where beams and columns form the primary structure. Steep by today's standards, the ramp of this inclined section is more than a means of circulation: it is a catalyst for the conceptual, organizational, and spatial articulation of the house.

V. C. Morris Gift Shop │ San Francisco, California, USA

The Morris Gift Shop, a precursor to Frank Lloyd Wright's design for the Solomon R. Guggenheim Museum, was built into an existing retail structure. The section indicates the insertion of the ramp, the tapered arched entrance, the curved first-floor ceiling, the second-floor partitions, and the acrylic, light-diffusing ceiling hung under the existing skylight. Wright's design for the small shop hinges on the figural shape of the circulation ramp. The circular 4-ft-wide (1.2 m) ramp recenters the space toward the half-glazed entry vestibule, and the hung bubble ceiling masks the

Frank Lloyd Wright | 1949

misalignment with an existing skylight. As a seductive object, the ramp entices shoppers to the main retail area on the second floor. Small apertures that puncture the side walls of the ramp reveal objects for sale, turning circulation into browsing. While the ramp provides continuity between the first and second floors, it also segments the first floor by isolating the back shopping space. This inclined section is an ornate stage for shopping set within the existing shell: a building within a building.

The Solomon R. Guggenheim Museum | New York, New York, USA

The main gallery of the Guggenheim Museum is an exemplary demonstration of an inclined section defining an entire building. Rising at a 3 percent grade and stretching more than 1/4 mi (0.4 km) in length, the continuous path expands in width as it moves upward, producing a conical void at the center of the museum and an inverted conical form on the exterior. A skylight supported by concrete ribs fills the 92-ft-high (28 m) atrium with daylight, while the continuous perimeter skylight enabled by recessions in the exterior profile was intended to backlight paintings to make them appear to float. The tapered concrete balcony and integral soffit conceal

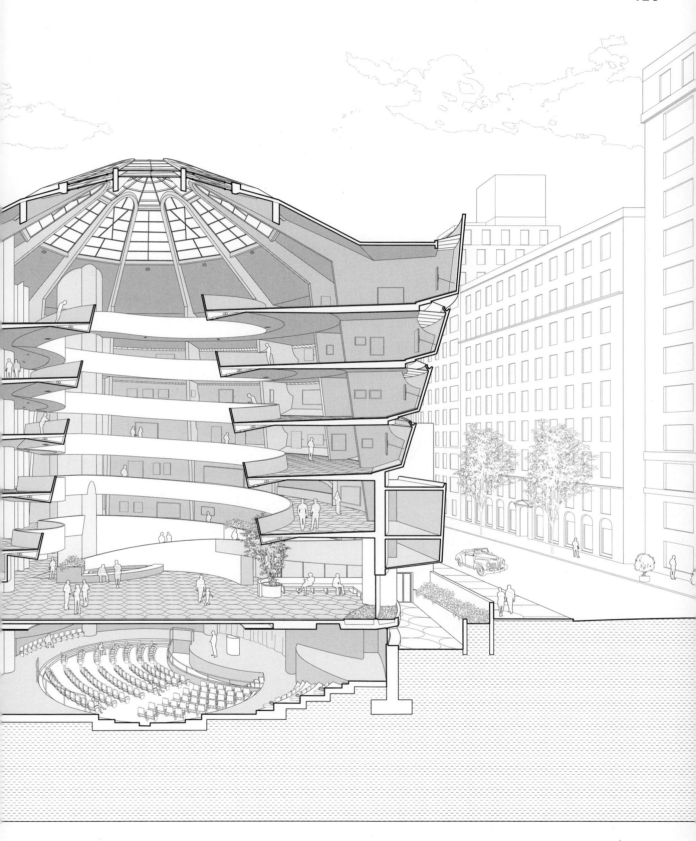

Frank Lloyd Wright | 1959

the air supply duct. The primary point of tension between the incline and level floor is at the bottom, where Wright folded the ramp up against itself to form a base. An exterior porte cochere separates the main gallery from the administrative wing. While the administrative wing echoes the circular form of the main gallery, the inclined section is confined to the gallery, as connection among the flat administrative floors is made through a service core, with a small atrium providing limited visible continuity. In the main gallery, the inclined section's physical continuity is complemented by the visual connectivity of the large atrium.

Incline — Shear — Stack

Kunsthal | Rotterdam, the Netherlands

Lodged against the edge of a dyke, the rectangular mass of this exhibit and events hall is bisected in two directions by site circulation. An inclined sidewalk connects the top of the dyke to the lower park, cutting an oblique path through the center of the building, while a road passes perpendicularly underneath that path. An abrupt entry is located at the joint between the incline of the exterior path and the incline of the auditorium. The intersection of inclined floors undermines the distinctions between above and below. The building unfolds as a continuous circuit that intensifies the disjunctions

OMA | 1992

produced by the bisecting site circulation. Reworking the unidirectional trope of the spiral museum, here the inclined surfaces of the circulation loop descend from the entry in the auditorium to a hall on the ground floor, ramp up to a second-floor gallery, and then, at the back of the auditorium, continue up elongated steps to a third-floor hall, which frames oblique views of the roofscapes across the dyke. The discontinuities in plan created by the inclined surfaces of this section are celebrated as they induce programmatic and volumetric friction along the circulation loop.

1111 Lincoln Road | Miami, Florida, USA

By intensifying the inclined section of a parking structure, the design of 1111 Lincoln Road transforms a garage for three hundred cars into a dynamic, open civic space, embracing the warm climate of Miami Beach. The new parking structure complements the simultaneous transformation of the adjacent 1970s SunTrust International Center from a bank into residences. Levels are linked through a sequence of ramps that facilitate the smooth passage of a car. Unlike the section of a typical parking structure, the floors of 1111 Lincoln Road are staggered to accommodate not only parking but also double- and triple-height spaces in which

Herzog & de Meuron | 2010

temporary events are staged, including photo shoots, yoga classes, and various other spectacles. Tapered concrete edges with small wire guardrails lighten the appearance of the structure, while figural V-shaped columns accentuate the varying heights of the floors. Nine different levels range from 8 to 34 ft (2.4 to 10.4 m) in height,

framing both narrow and expansive vistas over Miami. Retail spaces at the ground level engage the pedestrian Lincoln Road Mall, a fifth-floor fashion boutique animates the sculptural staircase, and a penthouse restaurant and private residence at the top complete the promenade of this inclined section.

Moesgaard Museum | Aarhus, Denmark

This museum of archaeology and ethnography is designed to be embedded in, and to emerge from, the very landscape that is the source of much of its collection. Visitors enter this artificial hill through its side into a foyer located at the midpoint of a very large stair, which leads to galleries on three levels.

The dominant feature of the building is its ten-degree, oblique, inhabitable green roof, which is contiguous on one side with the more gently sloping terrain. The slope of the building provides panoramic views and an inclined surface for picnics or sledding. The underside of this incline is legible as a continuous wood

slat ceiling, which defines the major spaces within the building. This sloped surface is recessed and leveled out near its base to provide optical and physical links between inside and out. The building is a horizontal shear of stacked galleries, which is both overlaid with and intersected by an inclined roof.

Nests produce sections through interplay or overlap between discrete volumes. While Stack, Shear, Hole, and Incline work primarily with flat plates, a Nest positions three-dimensional figures in specific relationships for sectional consequences. The spatial, structural, or environmental performance of the nest usually exceeds that of the volumes operating in isolation.

NEST

Villa Moller | Vienna, Austria

Adolf Loos's approach to domestic architecture through the clustering of rooms in complex and staggered relationship to one another, referred to as *Raumplan*, is an example of a nested architectural section. Rather than occupying floor plates, rooms are afforded distinct spatial positions within the volume and section of the house, enabled by the flexibility of wood stick framing. Rooms are tied to one another and anchored to load-bearing exterior walls. Villa Moller comprises a music salon, dining room, library, atelier, and five bedrooms, with entry and service spaces in the ground floor. The masklike, symmetrical front facade hides the

Adolf Loos | 1928

complexity of the interior sequence and sections. Though it is only four stories tall, Villa Moller has eight level changes, which stage an intricate sequence of relationships among stasis, movement, activity, and views. In particular, the dining room and music salon are distinguished by three retractable steps within an opening between the two rooms that frames the activity occurring in each. Perpendicular to this pairing is the view from the built-in bench above the front door, which passes obliquely down through the music room to the garden beyond. Staircases wind through and engage the sequence of rooms, animating the nested section.

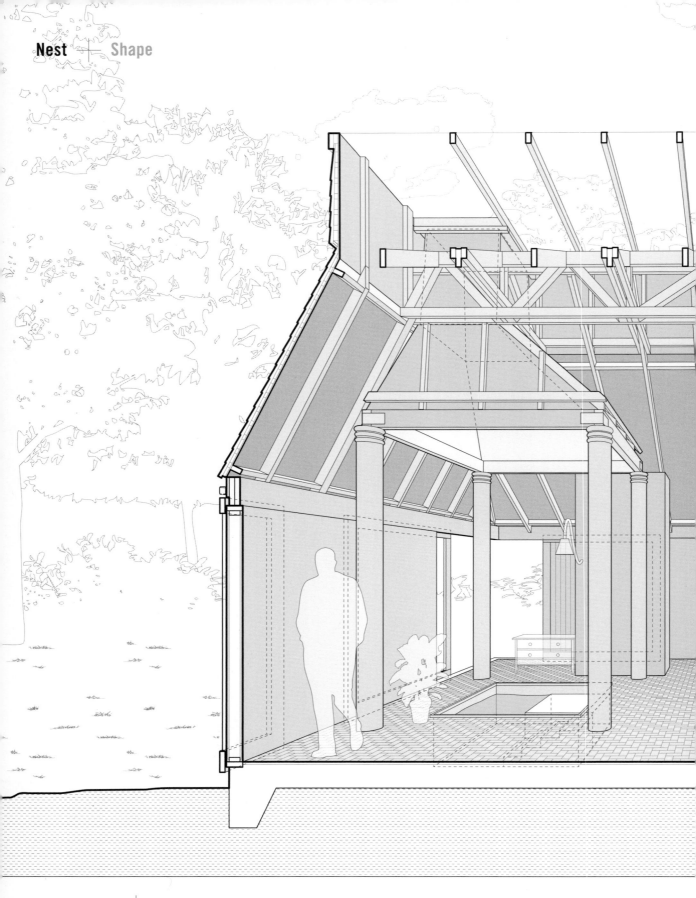

Moore House | Orinda, California, USA

Charles Moore designed this house for himself, nesting a series of unique spaces within a tight 26-ft-8-in (8.1 m) square footprint. Two sets of four wood columns capped by tapered wood funnels sit asymmetrically in the square plan. These aedicules are open to the roof, capped with skylights and painted white on the inside, illuminating the framed domestic spaces of the sunken tub and the living room. Only a few nonstructural partitions break up the interior space, enclosing a closet and water closet in the back. A unifying roof made from standard dimensional lumber tops the four exterior

Charles Moore | 1962

walls. Only half of each these perimeter walls is rooted in place, while the remaining halves are composed of wood and glass panels that are hung on tracks; these can slide over the static walls to open up all four corners of the house. With no structure in the corners, the logic of this nested section provides the structure of the house, as the eight interior columns lock into a wood truss spanning the high point of the roof. Through the use of a nested section, the house achieves a theatricality and complexity within a small volume of space.

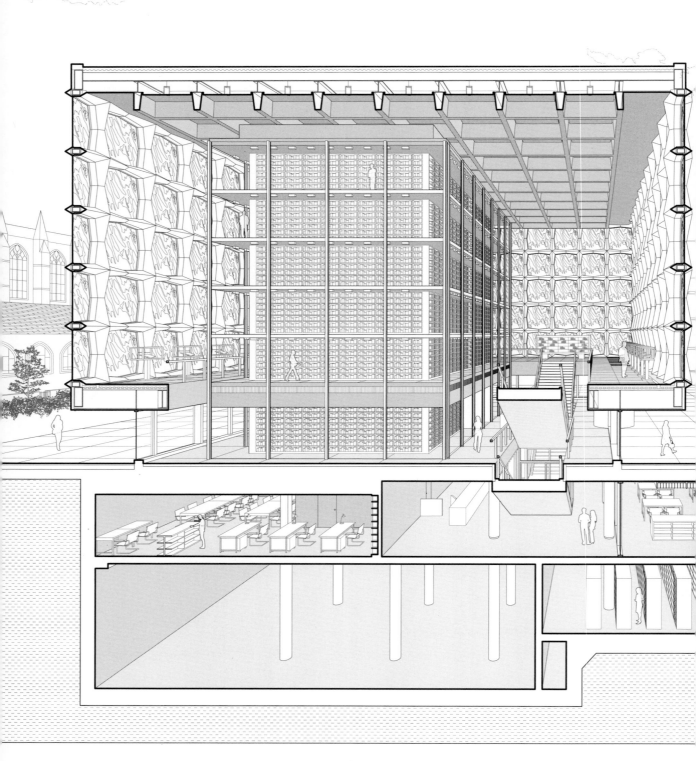

Beinecke Rare Book and Manuscript Library | New Haven, Connecticut, USA

The rare book and manuscript library at Yale University demonstrates the capacity of inset nesting to modulate light and climate through a multilayered construction. The outer box is composed of four steel Vierendeel truss walls, clad in faceted stone and precast concrete. The grid formed by the trusses is inset with 1-1/4-in-thick (3.2 cm) translucent marble panels that filter out ultraviolet rays while providing indirect illumination. The stone container is juxtaposed with an inner box composed of a steel structure and glass panels that provide precise thermal and climatic control. This glass box allows the tower of fragile books to be

Gordon Bunshaft of Skidmore, Owings & Merrill | 1963

placed on full view, yet within a highly controlled environment. An exhibition mezzanine wraps around the nested volume. The walls transfer structural load to four points at the corners, where pillars elevate the stone enclosure off the ground, making the outer frame seem to float monumentally above the stone plaza in the heart of the campus. A sunken courtyard provides daylight to underground offices and library facilities. While the nested section produces the spectacle of this library, excavated space below contains the primary support facilities for the display above, including seminar rooms, offices, curatorial spaces, and the vast majority of the books.

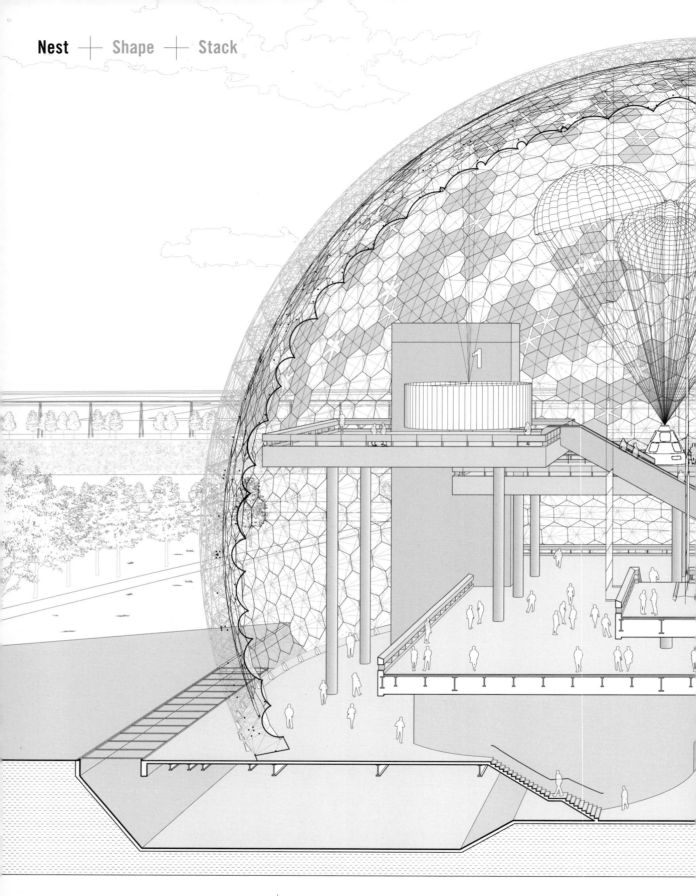

United States Pavilion at Expo '67 | Montreal, Canada

This pavilion was commissioned at the height of the Cold War by the United States Information Agency to stand opposite the Soviet Pavilion. The American Pavilion contained a three-hundred-seat theater and multilevel exhibition platforms designed by Cambridge Seven Associates to celebrate the country's cultural and aeronautical achievements. All exhibition spaces were nested inside a geodesic steel-framed dome with a diameter of 250 ft (76.2 m) and a height of 206 ft (62.8 m). A 40-in (101.6 cm) gap separated the outer triangulated surface of the dome from an inner hexagonal surface, which was infilled with 1/4-in-thick (6.4 mm)

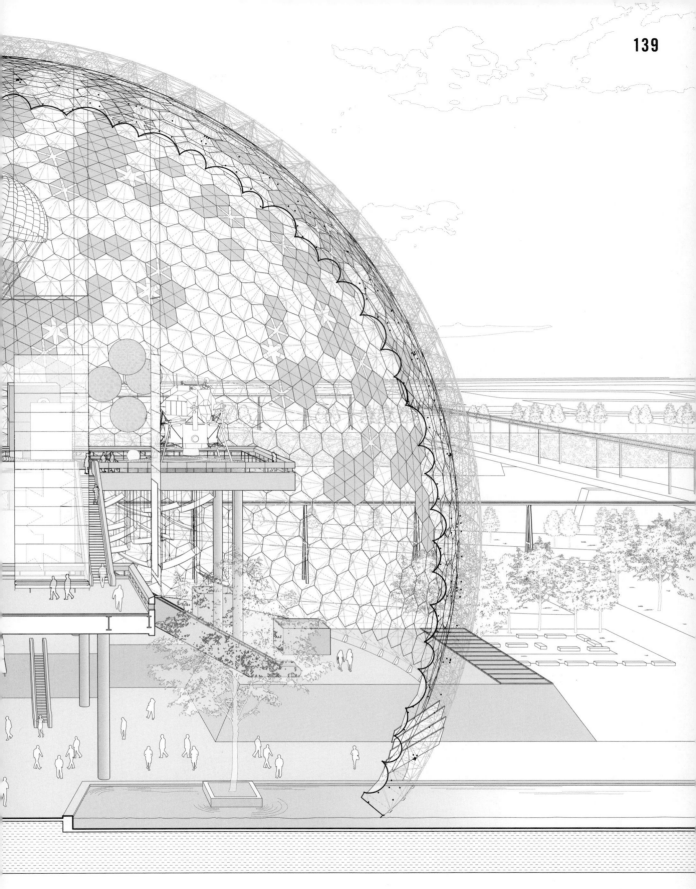

Buckminster Fuller and Shoji Sadao | 1967

transparent acrylic panels. A motorized, self-regulating shading system covered one-third of the panels, working with air-conditioning to create a vast thermal microclimate. Within the interior volume of 6.7 million cu ft (189,722 cu m) were a series of concrete platforms supported by rolled-steel sections and 30-in-diameter (76.2 cm) steel columns. These exhibition trays were accessed via a series of escalators, one of which was 125 ft (38.1 m) long—at the time the longest ever constructed. This unique space was a consequence of the radical difference between the occupiable horizontal platforms and the huge translucent dome.

Nest

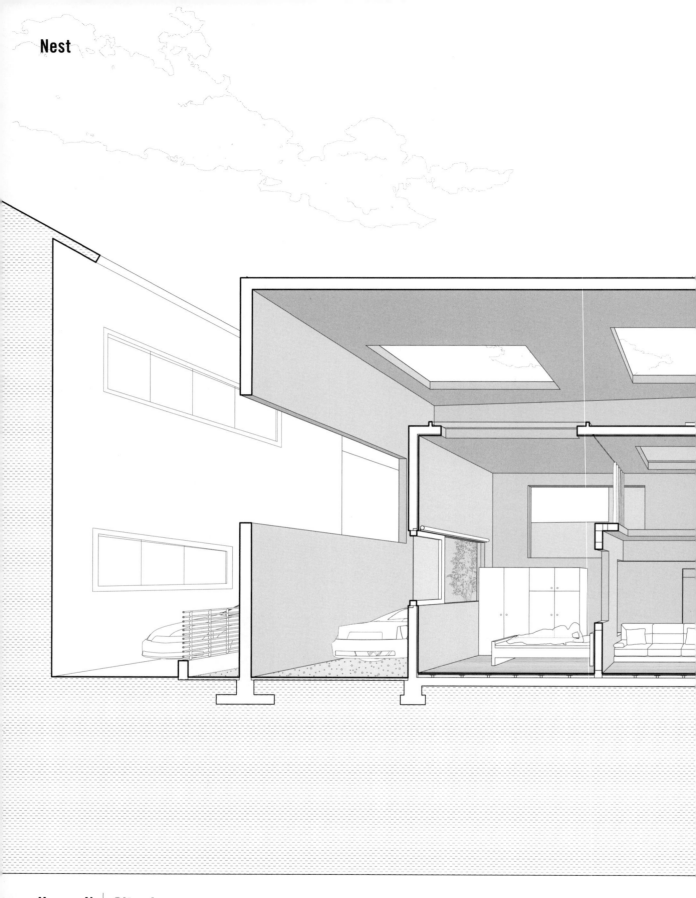

House N | Oita, Japan

Sou Fujimoto's design for this single-family house uses a series of three nested boxes, each punctured by large rectangular apertures, to configure the interior and exterior of the house. Each box plays a distinct role in the architectural enclosure. The innermost box, made from lightweight wood and plaster, separates the living and dining functions at the center from the bedroom and ceremonial spaces around its perimeter. The middle box, constructed in concrete with glass windows, provides the weather and thermal enclosure. The outermost concrete shell delineates the property boundary

Sou Fujimoto Architects | **2008**

and creates a screen of privacy in the gardens for residents' outdoor activities while filtering sunlight. Moving outward from shell to shell, the thickness of the walls increases from 5 7/16 in (13.8 cm) to 7 1/16 in (18 cm) to 8 11/16 in (22 cm), growing proportionally by structural necessity. Only kitchen and bathroom, which are set between the outer and middle shells and bounded by glass side partitions, challenge the successive logic of this building's nested section.

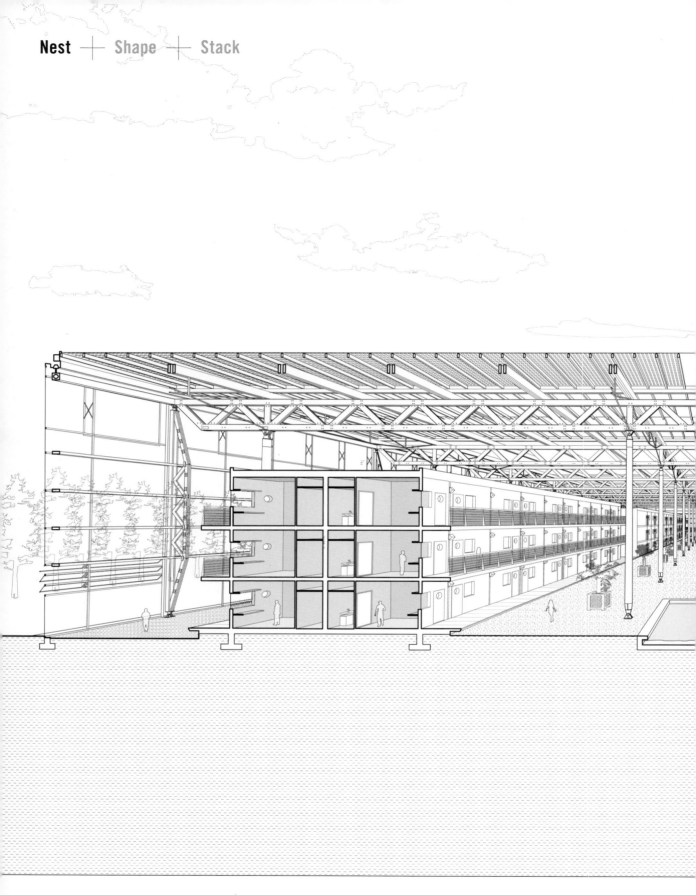

Mont-Cenis Training Center | Herne-Sodingen, Germany

Built over the head of the abandoned Mont-Cenis coal mine, this civil-service facility demonstrates how a nested section can generate temperature gradients through microenvironments at an urban scale. Two rows of two- and three-story structures, designed to support short-term training and educational facilities, sit underneath a vast 123,000-sq-ft (11,427 sq m) glass envelope. Built from locally manufactured glass and regionally harvested timber, this solar greenhouse floats on 50-ft-tall (15.2 m) timber poles and is spanned by laminated wood trusses carrying 100,000 sq ft (9,290 sq m) of photovoltaic panels that generate two and a half times

Jourda Architectes | 1999

the energy consumed by the complex. Motorized openings at the upper and lower quadrants of the glazed box induce a controlled stack effect to modulate a temperate interior microclimate year-round. Pools and vegetation provide cooling while populating the gardens and courtyards of this campus-in-a-terrarium. Freed of the requirement for extensive weather enclosure or insulation, the educational structures were inexpensive to build. In this nested section the interstitial space is neither exterior nor fully interior, but provides an inhabitable, passively conditioned buffer zone, enhancing the performance of the buildings within.

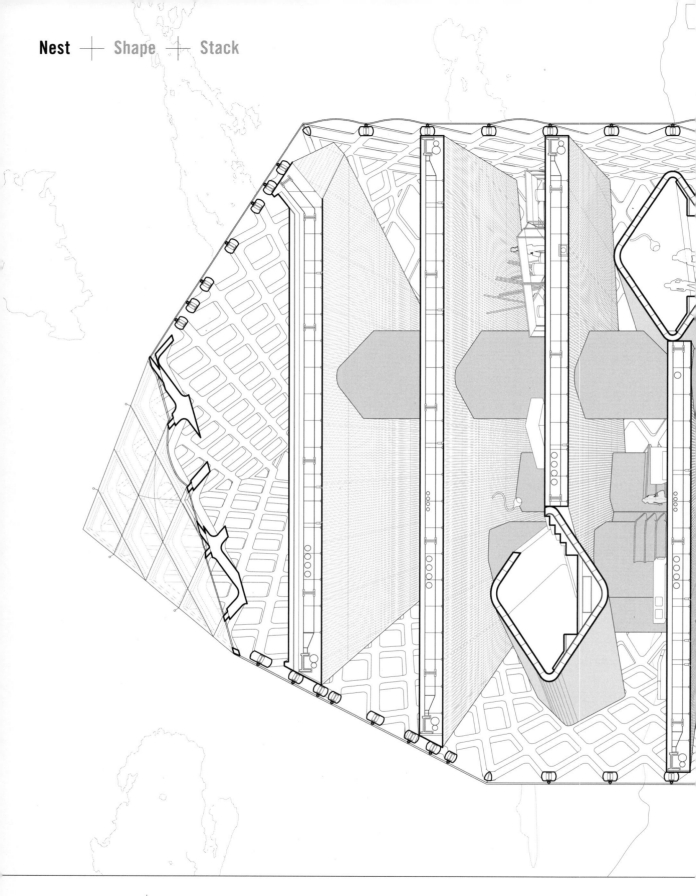

Prada Aoyama | Tokyo, Japan

The Prada flagship store in Tokyo combines an overall figural shape with inset stacked floors and nested tubes to create a steel and glass shopping icon. A structural exoskeleton made from 7-1/16–by–8-1/16-in (18 by 20.5 cm) steel I-sections welded on site and encased in a fire-resistant layer of calcium

silicate form a grid of rhomboids, each 10 ft 6 in by 6 ft 6 in (3.2 by 2 m). Within the diagonal frame, convex, concave, and flat glass pillows provide a consistently varied texture to the building envelope, which comprises ten faceted sides. The entire building is set into a concrete tub, where isolation mats stabilize the structure

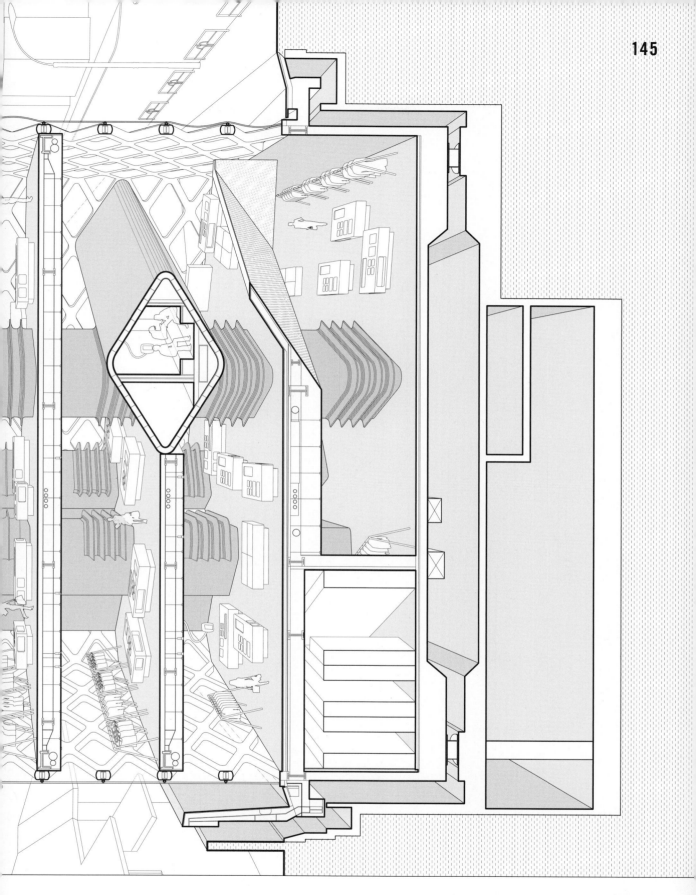

Herzog & de Meuron | 2003

during earthquakes. Inside, seven regularly spaced concrete floor slabs span from the exterior skin and interior circulation cores and conceal mechanical and electrical distribution. Three horizontal tubes, aligned with groups of four rhomboids on the facade, are nested in the floor plates. These tubes enclose areas for changing and checkout and provide lateral stability. Extruded from the diagrid facade, yet embedded within the figural building volume and bifurcating floors, these nested spaces complicate distinctions between exterior and interior or from floor to floor, producing an intricate fusion of skin, structure, space, and form.

De Effenaar | Eindhoven, the Netherlands

The design for this youth music center bundles a set of discrete rectangular volumes to create a multifunctional venue. Each volume, enclosed in reinforced concrete, holds a particular function or program, from a small stage to changing rooms to recording spaces and cafes. Pushed to the periphery of the section, these boxes collectively form a single rectangle when seen in elevation. The residual space in the inside comprises the main performance venue. The walls of the fifth floor double as structural beams spanning the open performance space below, transferring loads to the north and south. Overlapping

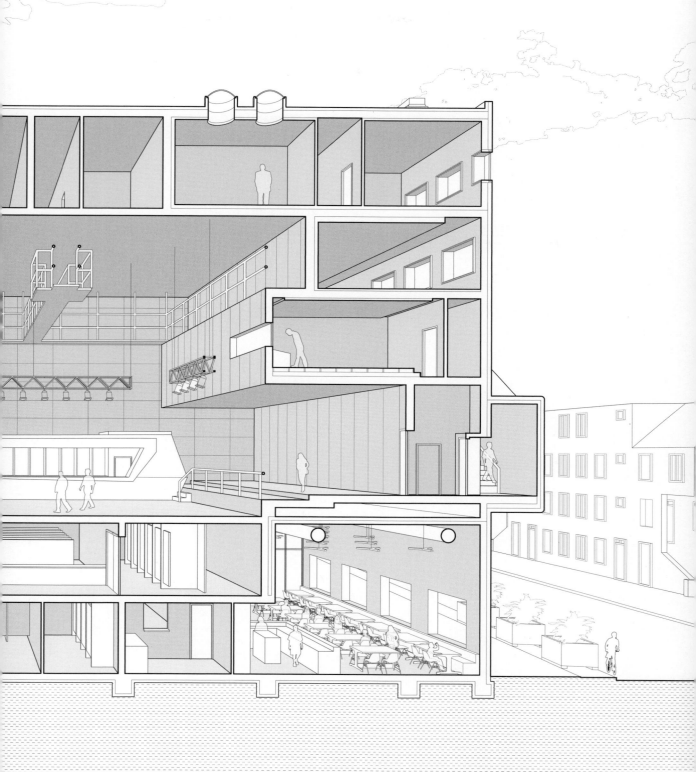

MVRDV | 2005

and misaligned boxes create balcony spaces and projection rooms, linked together by a supplementary catwalk. Circulating and egress stairs are appended to the outside of the main volume, establishing an iconic twisting figure on an otherwise undistinguished box, while enabling a tight nesting of volumes in section.

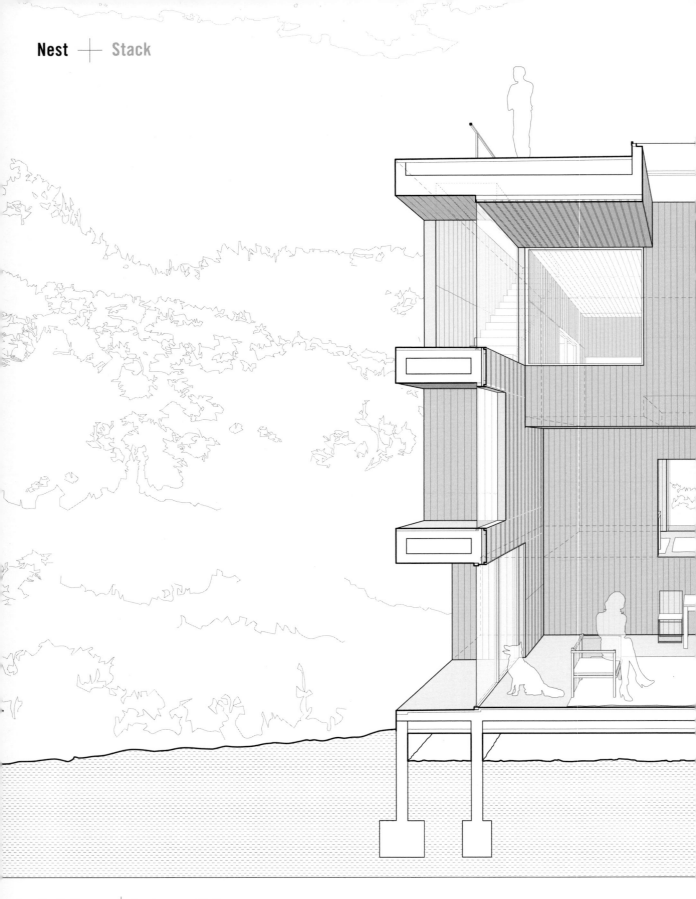

Poli House | Coliumo, Chile

Set on the side of a remote cliff, the Poli House is an enigmatic perforated sculptural cube that evades quick apprehension of scale and use. 6-ft-6-in (2 m) square punches in its concrete shell reveal a rich layering of structure, skins, and nested volumes. This vacation house / cultural center is organized

as a cube within a cube, producing a 3-ft-3-in-wide (1 m) perimeter. Although this redundancy of layers would typically intensify distinctions between the interior and the exterior, here the thickness of that perimeter produces more complex readings. Calibrated for shading and weather protection, exterior glazing is located on both sides of this perimeter.

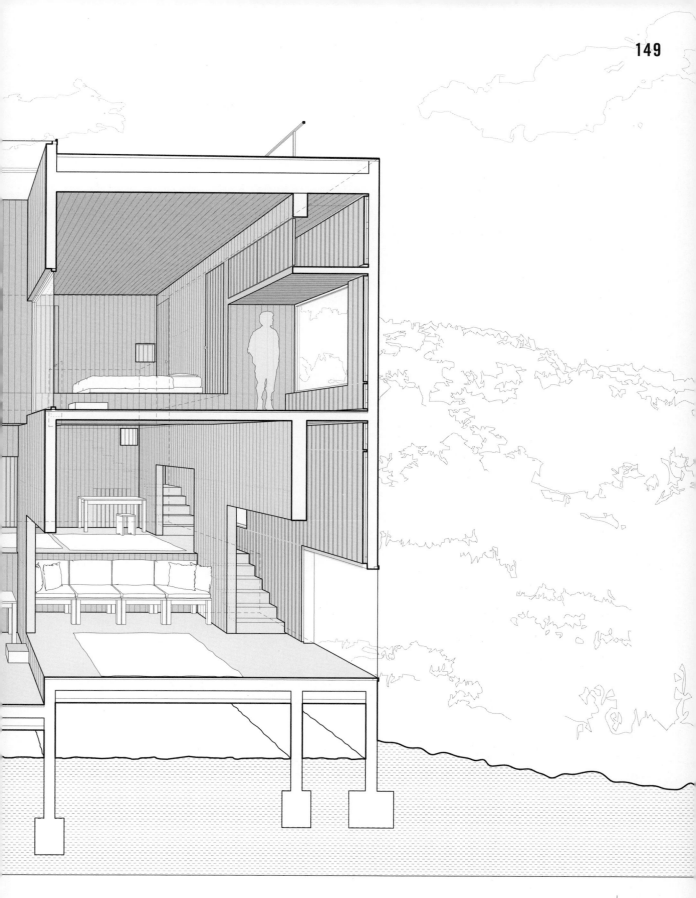

Pezo von Ellrichshausen | 2005

zone, making its space both exterior and interior. This occupiable perimeter houses all the service spaces, including a kitchenette, bathrooms, and staircases. The furniture can be stored in closets, with the perimeter freeing the remaining nested interior volumes for a range of uses, from living room to bedroom to study. Linked by a series of oversize apertures, these rooms spiral up counterclockwise around the central three-story living space, creating a house with six distinct levels. The wood boards used as formwork during construction were reused as interior cladding for walls and furniture, blurring the distinction between skin and structure.

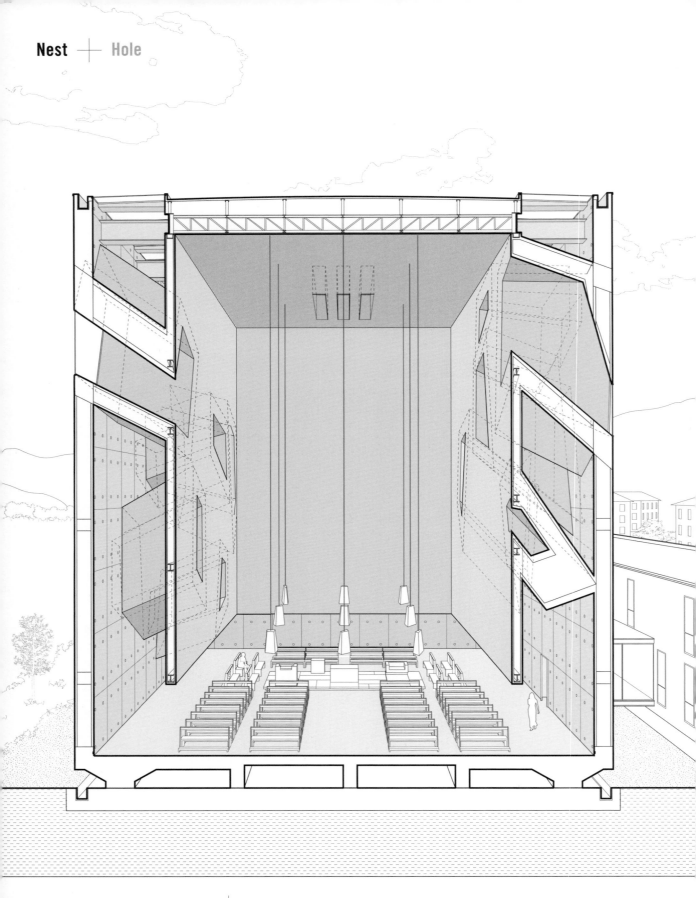

San Paolo Parish Complex │ Foligno, Italy

The San Paolo Parish Complex uses nested enclosures to create structural resiliency and to orchestrate lighting effects within a sequence of concentric volumes. The complex replaces a house of worship destroyed by an earthquake. Standing 82 ft (25 m) high on a 98-ft-5-in—by—73-ft-10-in

(30 by 22.5 m) footprint, the outer volume provides the primary structural system of a cast-in-place concrete box resting on the ground. Floating just above head height, the inner lightweight steel box rendered in plaster is suspended from steel beams that frame the top of the concrete box. The

Studio Fuksas | 2009

inner space is tethered to the outer structure by trapezoidal tubes that draw discrete zones of daylight toward the altar. Extensive skylights between the two shells accentuate their material differences, while establishing contrast between the darker inner church and the more generously illuminated peripheral ring. The effect of this nested section is to reinforce the sacred function of the minimally furnished sequence of spaces within the building.

Nest

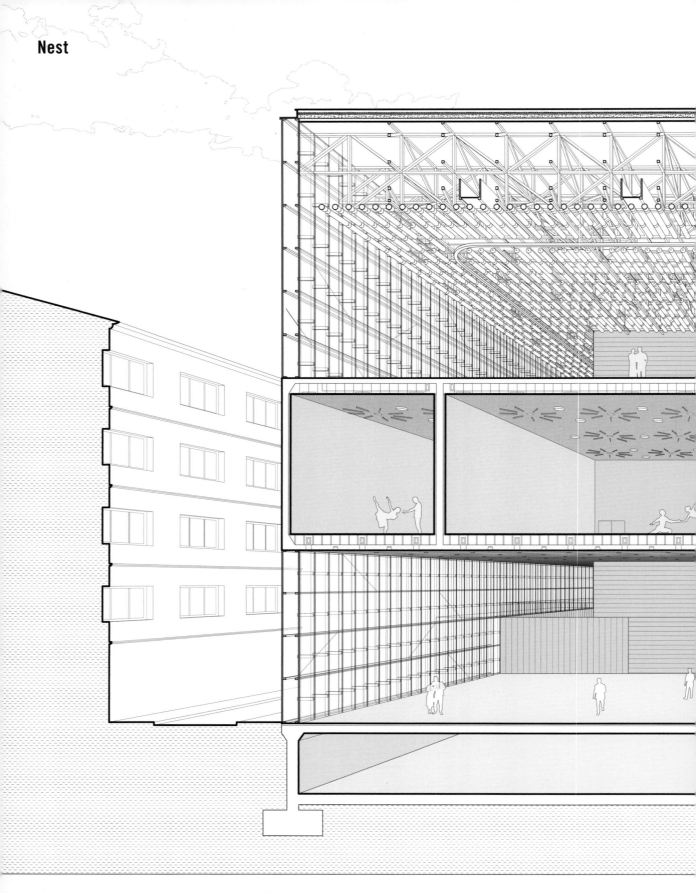

Center for the Arts in La Coruña | La Coruña, Spain

As this drawing shows, this arts facility was originally imagined as two intertwining institutions—a dance conservatory and a public museum—nested within a single steel-framed, insulated glass box. Spaces related to the dance conservatory, accessible only to students and staff, were located inside discrete concrete volumes connected by a vertical circulation core. Pushed to the exterior, these volumes read as recognizable figures caught within the building's double skin. The public museum was to be located on the floors formed by the tops of the dance conservatory volumes. The two programs were to remain autonomous, a division

aceboXalonso Studio | 2011

reinforced by differences in materiality and illumination. Multicolored acoustic tubes hung from the ceiling to absorb sound from museumgoers and to conceal mechanical equipment and trusses. Dance studios lit by fluorescent bulbs and direct sunlight floated between galleries illuminated by diffused light. However, after ten years of construction and vacancy, the building opened with new tenants as the National Museum of Science and Technology. At that point, adjustments were made to combine the two separate spatial configurations into a single building, undermining the sectional bifurcation of programs in the original design.

Extrusion, Stack, Shape, Shear, Hole, Incline, and Nest are primary methods of operating in section. For the sake of clarity, they have been presented as distinct modes, but they rarely operate in isolation. Indeed, buildings exhibiting the most complex and intricate sections contain all manner of combinations and hybrids.

HYBRIDS

Villa Girasole | Marcellise, Italy

The main living spaces of Villa Girasole rotate to maintain an ideal relationship
between the house and the sun over the course of the day, thanks to a highly
engineered set of intertwined architectural and sectional devices. A semicircu-
lar solid masonry base is built into the hillside, retaining the sloped landscape
to create a circular terrace above. Comprising three main levels, this base serves
as a garage, lower-level entrance, and open-air ambulatory. An eight-story open,
circular staircase, designed to resemble a lighthouse, nests into the base and rises
to connect the two wings of main living spaces in the upper villa. Constructed with

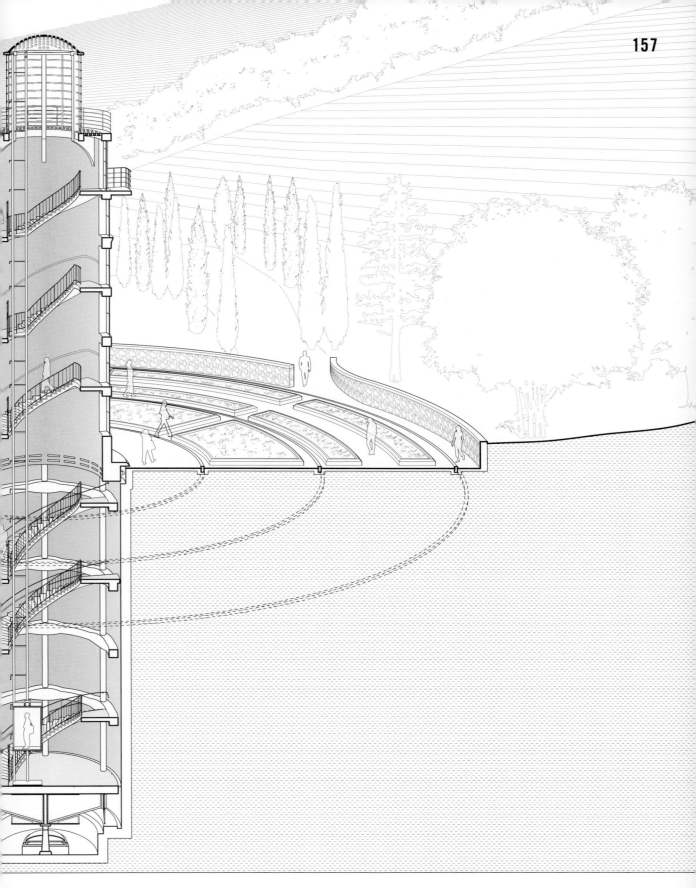

Angelo Invernizzi | 1935

a lightweight concrete frame clad in sheet metal, the entire upper level, including the staircase, rotates on fifteen wheels, powered by two motors, turning a full rotation in nine hours and twenty minutes. A thrust-block at the base of the 138-ft-11-in-high (42.35 m) staircase anchors the pivoting tower, while the ground above is inscribed as a formal garden to accommodate the circular motion. The angle of sunlight is altered only by the sun's changes in altitude, since the villa tracks its horizontal movement. The hybrid and dynamic section of Villa Girasole thus encompasses the sun by isolating the effects of its movements to section.

Stack ┼ Hole ┼ Shear ┼ Nest ┼ Shape

Yale Art and Architecture Building | New Haven, Connecticut, USA

Designed and constructed during Paul Rudolph's tenure as chair of the architecture department, the iconic Art and Architecture Building arrays 37 unique floor levels around a central core of open, collective spaces anchored by a series of striated-concrete towers. The section, which combines stacked,

sheared, and nested forms punctuated by holes, produces a variety of visual and spatial overlaps and intersections, most notably among the expansive central pinup spaces and galleries and the more peripheral and compressed studios and offices. Staggered levels, bridges, and offsets multiply the interactions among

Paul Rudolph | 1963

adjacent spaces while allowing for campus views through large, steel-framed glass windows from deep within the interior. Massive piers of heavily textured, bush-hammered concrete provide structural support for horizontal platforms, house mechanical services, and contain vertical circulation. At the upper levels, the play of horizontal planes gives way to enclosed tubelike forms that bridge the vertical masses to enclose the spaces below. Between these volumes a collection of skylights and clerestories admit daylight, enlivening the varied spaces of this complex combination of section types.

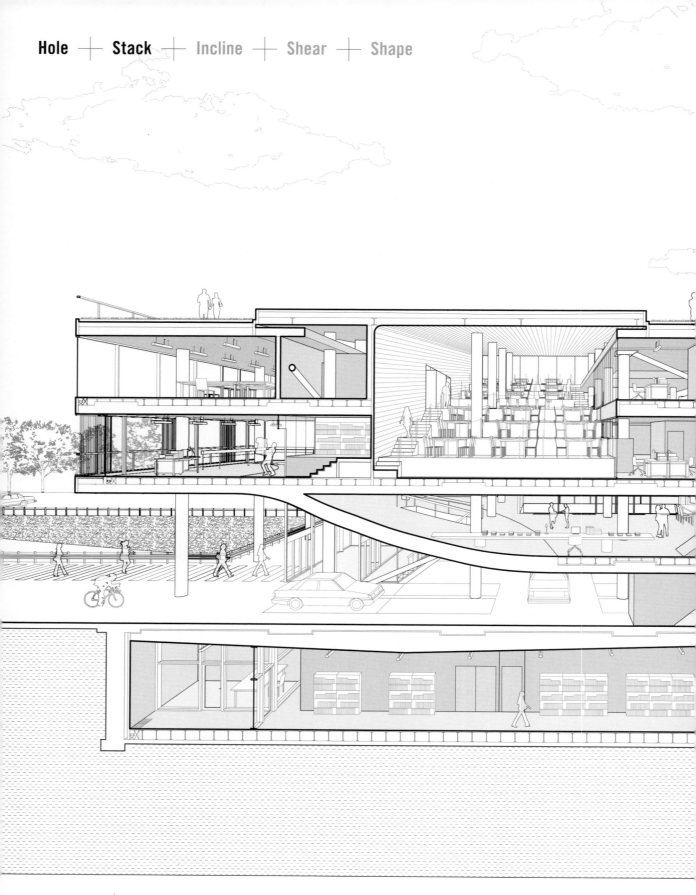

Villa VPRO | Hilversum, the Netherlands

The Villa VPRO challenges the homogeneity of stacked office buildings through a series of formal interventions. MVRDV's design for this broadcasting company's headquarters sought to maintain the idiosyncratic spatial configurations of VPRO's thirteen original office villas as they were consolidated into a single new construction. The project establishes a dialogue between the regularity of the square building footprint, with five concrete floors supported on a rectilinear column grid, and a series of moves that disrupt the generic form. The floor of the parking level curves back into its ceiling, creating a figural shape that animates the three-story central

MVRDV | **1997**

spine. Multiple holes throughout the project interrupt continuity of plan and provide sectional connections. Inclined planes link floors together, form a sunken courtyard connected to a roof garden, and serve as the sloped floor for a theater. Floor plates are sheared to create a stepped sequence of spaces and to distribute light and offer views. The spatial diversity and interwoven circulation paths that result from these interventions intensify the social interaction of the company. On all four elevations infill and recessed glazing reveal the concrete floor plates and cast the hybrid section as the iconic image of the building: the section as facade.

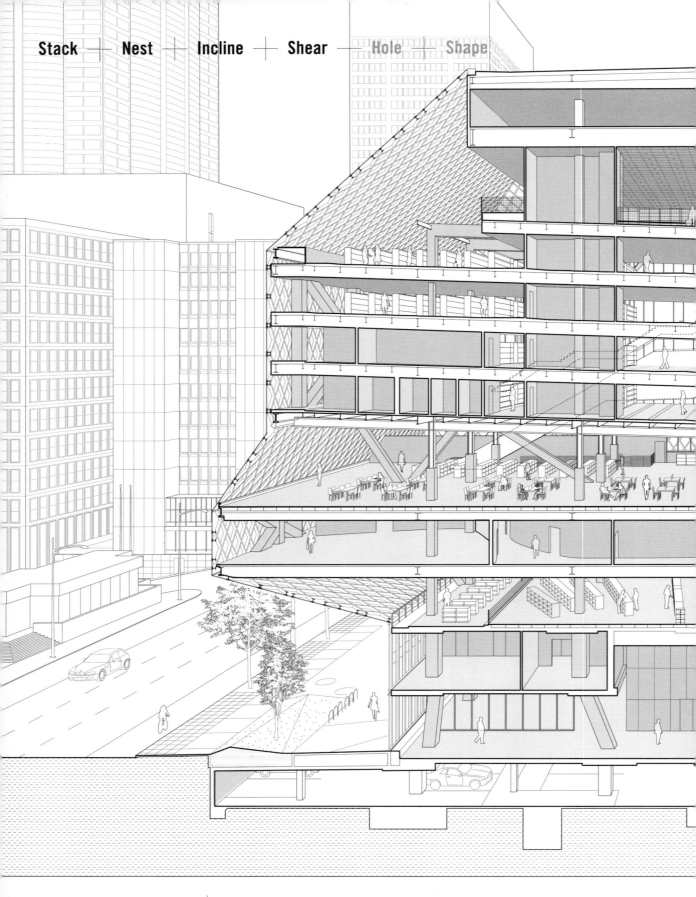

Stack ── Nest ── Incline ── Shear ── Hole ── Shape

Seattle Central Library | Seattle, Washington, USA

The design of the Seattle Central Library, which occupies an entire downtown city block, exemplifies the compatible intersection of different section types at multiple scales in clustered relationships. The project is organized by a stacking sequence that gathers similar functional areas within a continuous skin. The stable programs of administration and staff areas, book storage, meeting rooms, and parking are set within floor trays. These trays are offset vertically and slid horizontally as independent units in all four cardinal directions, creating atriums, exterior canopies, and self-shading overhangs. The most active spaces for reading and

OMA / LMN Architects | 2004

socializing are lodged between the stacked and shifted trays. Local sectional transformations are tailored to the unique functions of each tray. The four floors of bookstacks are inclined and united as a continuous spiral, facilitating the reorganization and expansion of the collection and turning browsing into an architectural promenade. An inclined auditorium intersects the staff space, providing visual continuity in alignment with the sloped urban site. A mesh facade structured by 1-ft-deep (30.5 cm) steel tubes aids in the transfer of lateral forces and creates a recognizable figure for the library.

Knowlton Hall | Columbus, Ohio, USA

This 176,000-sq-ft (16,350 sq m) architecture school organizes a programmatically diverse array of spaces within its figural campus footprint. Two
parallel ramped walkways run the length of the plan, beyond the length
required by circulation, linking and activating all the programs. The ramps

extend from the basement shop and auditorium past ground-floor galleries,
classrooms, and crit spaces; the second-floor ring of offices; the third-level
studios; and the top-level library and computer rooms, finally culminating
in an exterior rooftop garden. The ramps mark an area of discontinuity in plan

Mack Scogin Merrill Elam Architects | 2004

and continuity in section, providing an opportunity for the floor levels to vertically shear. The concrete structure, clad in marble shingles, is willfully carved away for glass-lined courtyards in and under the building mass. Double-height spaces enliven the interior. Horizontal and vertical shears, atriums, nested volumes, and, most important, inclined surfaces are all deployed to facilitate social exchanges. As a result, the building serves as a teaching instrument, demonstrating the pleasures and possibilities of space animated through section.

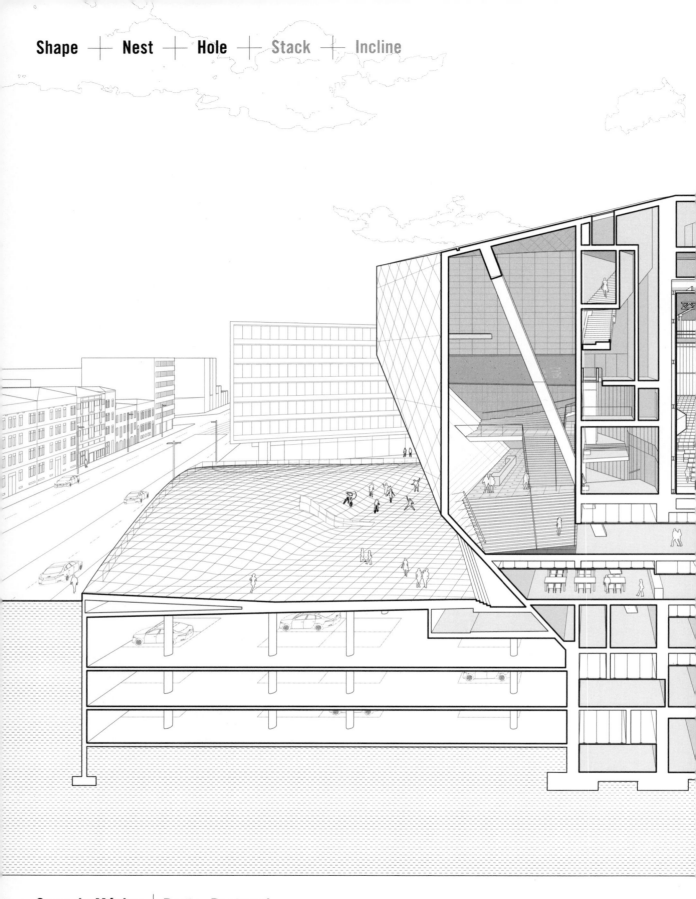

Casa da Música | Porto, Portugal

Because shoe box–shaped concert halls provide superior acoustics but lack architectural interest, OMA's Casa da Música nests a rectangular concert hall inside a padding of mixed programs occupying a faceted envelope. The main concert hall of the Casa da Música was conceived as a void, a hole in the center of the complex. Ancillary support and circulation spaces line the perimeter of the hall, each space's section dictated by function. To one side, the main ceremonial staircase ascends a towering atrium. Smaller recording studios and recital halls are given stepped floors and tapered sections. Below the belly, boxlike practice rooms,

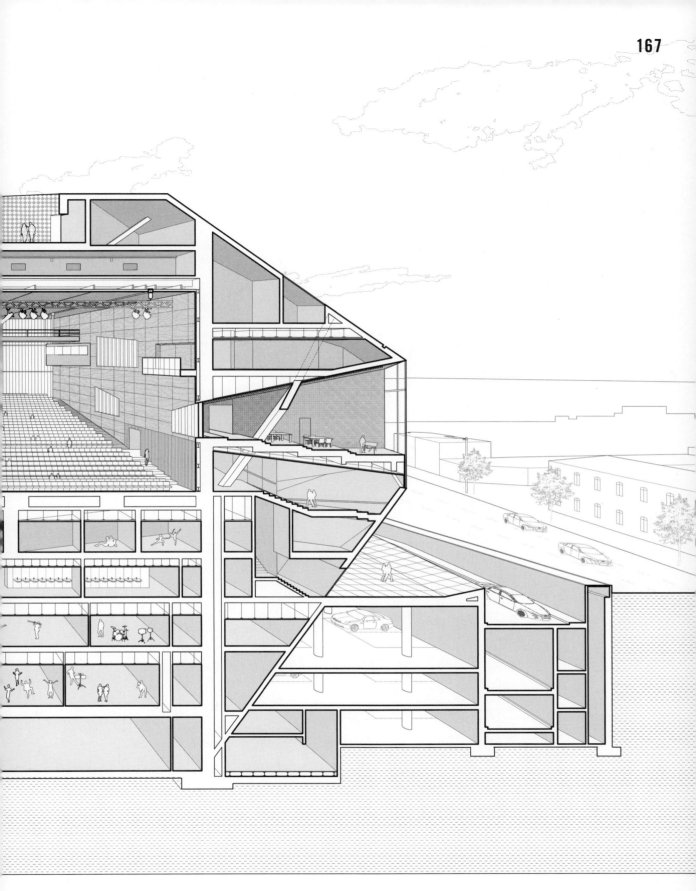

OMA | 2005

dance halls, and rehearsal venues nest among the structural frames that support the void created by the concert hall. A multifaceted stone skin angles in as it meets the ground, reinforcing the objecthood of this building that sits alone in the center of its site. Apertures aligned with the ends of the acoustic box of the performance hall are clad in double layers of curved glass, revealing to the city the activity within. In this hybrid section, an extensive belowground parking facility, constructed as an independent slab structure, mitigates vibration and creates the topographic stone surface into which the building as shaped and curious object is set.

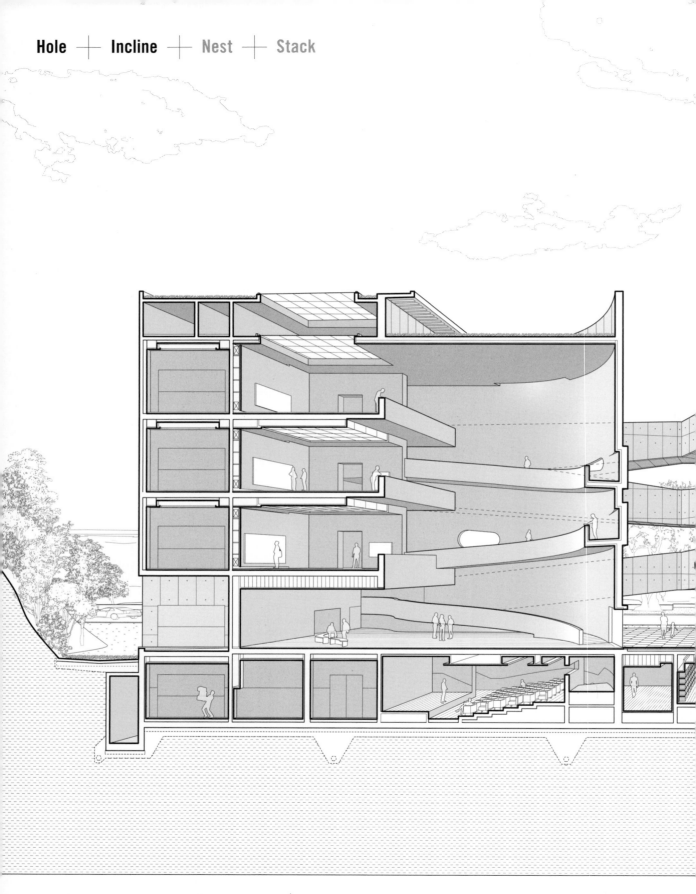

Iberê Camargo Foundation Museum | Porto Alegre, Brazil

This cultural building occupies a narrow site between a coastal highway and a densely vegetated cliff. In this confined site, Siza situated a partly subterranean linear plinth and a sculptural volume of white reinforced concrete. The plinth contains various programs, including an archive, an auditorium, and parking located underneath the road. Containing the primary exhibition space, the sculptural volume is defined by a series of L-shaped, top-lit rectilinear galleries framing a four-story atrium wrapped on the side opposite the galleries by a series of undulating circulation ramps. Together, these form a continuous promenade that weaves between

Álvaro Siza | 2008

interior and exterior. While the internal ramps nest against the sinuously shaped outer wall, the external ramps reach beyond the face of the building in concrete tubes, delineating an exterior entry court caught between the outer wall of the atrium and the cantilevered arms of the ramps. Like Frank Lloyd Wright's Guggenheim,

Siza's building couples the inclined surfaces of a ramping circulation system with the vertical organization of an atrium. In this hybrid section, however, the space enclosed extends outside the main volume of the building, linking the museum to its seaside site.

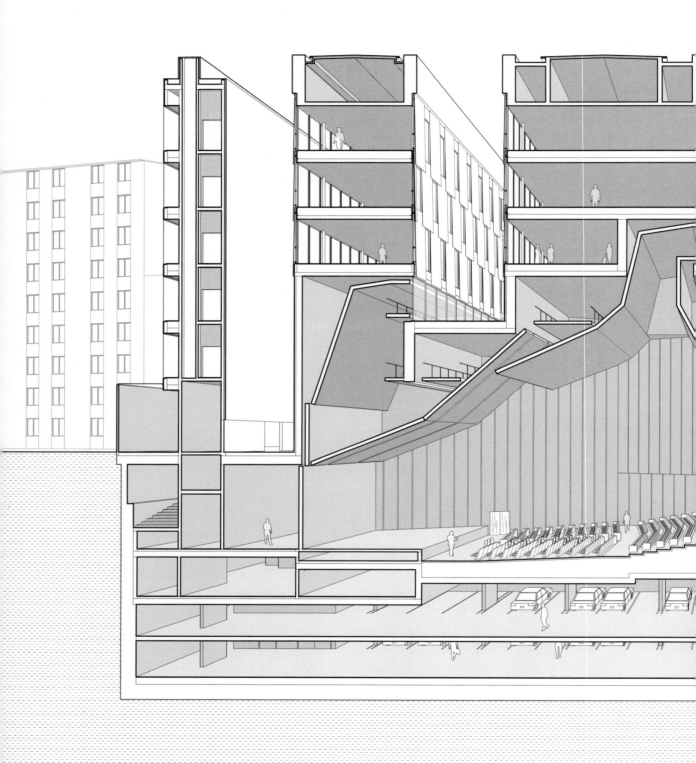

Università Luigi Bocconi │ Milan, Italy

By layering a gradient of variously permeable spaces, Grafton Architects' design for Università Luigi Bocconi met the competition challenge of integrating a programmatically diverse academic building within Milan's urban fabric. The 700,000-sq-ft (65,032 sq m) building, which includes conference halls, theaters, meeting rooms, and offices for a thousand professors, fills the entire 262-ft-6-in-by-524-ft-11-in (80 by 160 m) site. The design of the complex is carefully attuned to daylight, using an open weave of structure to allow light to penetrate from the top and sides of the building. The raked

Grafton Architects | 2008

auditorium sits partially below grade, above two stacked layers of parking. Bands of faculty offices are hung perpendicularly to the auditorium with open spaces between. Gaps in the shaped ceiling of the auditorium act as sun scoops, drawing indirect light deep into the structure. In this hybrid section, the glass-framed entrance is sheared in relationship to the street, animating views into the lobby, which is wedged under the rake of the auditorium's seats, and reinforcing the visual relationship between the university and the city.

Shape ┼ Stack ┼ Nest

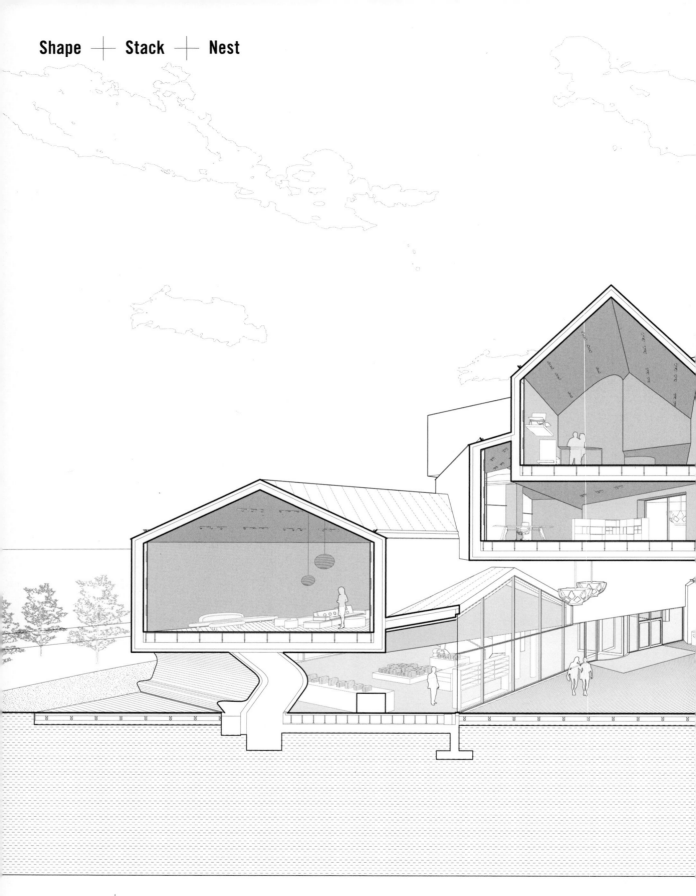

VitraHaus | Weil am Rhein, Germany

In this building, twelve volumes are stacked and nested to create a five-story-tall conference and exhibition center dedicated to the display of Vitra furniture. Each volume is a stretched extrusion of the iconic sectional profile of the prototypical gable-roofed house, creating a domestic scale for the presentation of furniture. The volumes are rotated and slid in relationship to each other. Where they intersect, new forms arise inside the section. Sculptural curved staircases provide vertical circulation, and a single elevator skewers the assembled volumes, creating a unique point of vertical continuity. The volumes are structural tubes,

Herzog & de Meuron | 2009

made from 9-7/8-in and 11-3/4-in (25 cm and 30 cm) site-cast concrete; they are open at the ends to frame views of the Vitra campus and the landscape beyond. The ends of all the elevated volumes are cantilevered, extending 49 ft (14.9 m) in the longest instance. The sides of the lowest volume appear to deflect under the weight of the others and are angled to conform to the back of a seat that accommodates visitors as they wait for entry. With its stacked, gable-shaped units, the building produces not only an intricate interior sequence but a faceted exterior atrium.

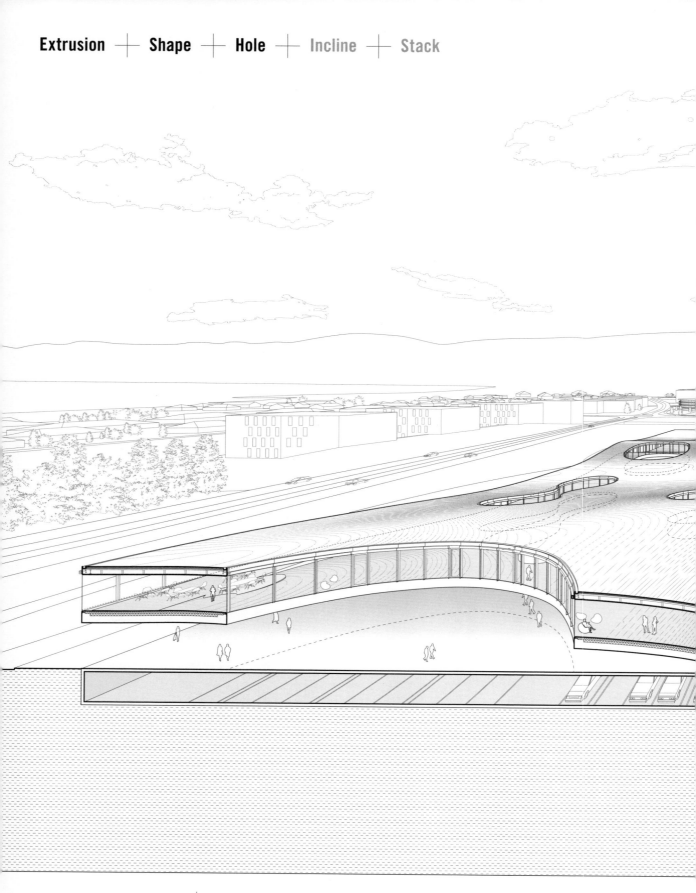

Rolex Learning Center | Lausanne, Switzerland

Located in the middle of an open site, this campus center for the École polytech-nique fédérale de Lausanne contains an array of social spaces, libraries, cafes, and meeting halls within a single, largely horizontal volume. The floor is a 2-ft-thick (61 cm) concrete slab, formed into a curved shell that lifts above the

ceiling of a subterranean parking structure, allowing the grounds of the campus to extend below and through the building. A 29-ft-6-in-by-29-ft-6-in (9 by 9 m) grid of slender steel columns supports a steel and glulam framed ceiling above the undulating slab. This building can be seen as a hybrid of three section types. Its rectangular,

SANAA | 2010

546-ft-3-in—by—398-ft-7-in (166.5 by 121.5 m) floor plate is extruded, typically, to a 10-ft-10-in (3.3 m) internal ceiling height, with a slightly higher extrusion for certain programs, such as performance halls. That extruded horizontal space is defined by two arched zones that delaminate from the ground and allow a clustering or puddling of programs on their shaped surfaces. This extrusion is then punctured by fourteen curvilinear holes, which distribute light and views obliquely through the slab. The cumulative effect of this hybrid section is the unprecedented spatial quality of a continuous free plan warped into the vertical axis.

Asakusa Culture and Tourism Center | Tokyo, Japan

This eight-story structure containing services for tourists is directly adjacent to the primary entry of Tokyo's historic Asakusa shrine. The building evokes a stack of wooden houses placed one on top of another to generate the vertical form of a tower. The unique form of each of these volumes, framed in structural steel, is shaped to reflect the nature of its program—with a double-height space for entry, sloping floors for an auditorium, and stacked meeting spaces expressed on the exterior as variously angled and horizontal planes. The spaces between the shaped ceiling of one volume and the floor of the

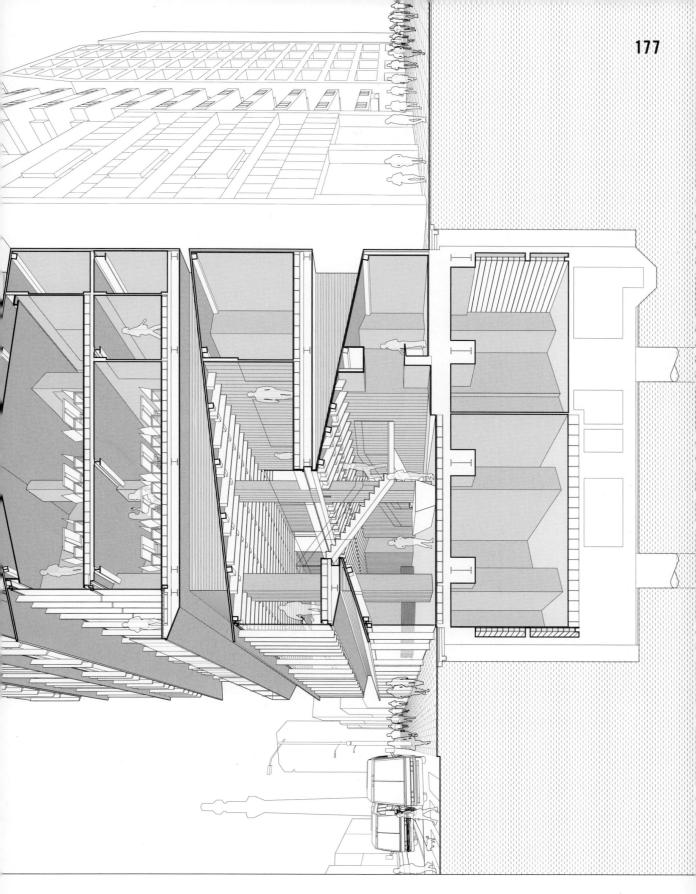

Kengo Kuma & Associates | 2012

next house technical equipment and storage, allowing the floor plans to remain largely unencumbered. These interstitial service zones are treated as recessed spandrels between each pair of volumes, creating a clear distinction between levels. While the stacked volumes, with their independent geometries and varying plan configurations, create a sense of stratification, a continuous screen of cedar fins unifies the exterior of this stacked and shaped section while providing sun shading and syncopated views of the city beyond.

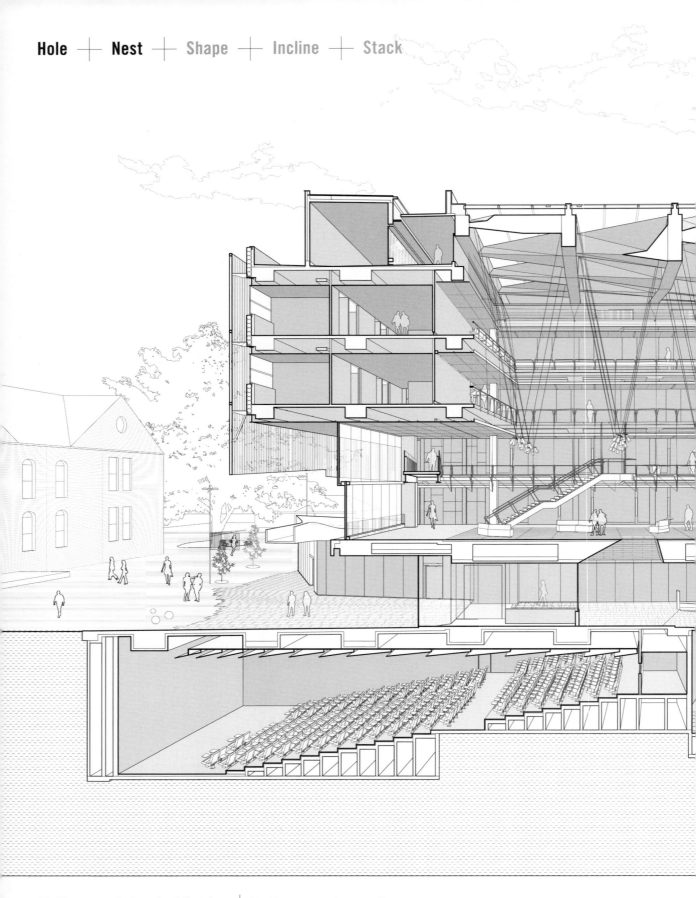

Melbourne School of Design | Melbourne, Australia

Continuing a tradition of schools of architecture that embody pedagogy, the
School of Design at the University of Melbourne combines a diverse range of
sectional strategies, structural systems, and formal and material plays. At the
ground level, a library and fabrication lab flank a broad internal promenade

visually and spatially linked to the campus. Above, classrooms, studios, and
research spaces are organized in two main wings around a central elevated atrium
that acts as drafting, exhibition, and event space. This multistory void is ringed
by circulation zones incorporating work surfaces and seating areas that provide

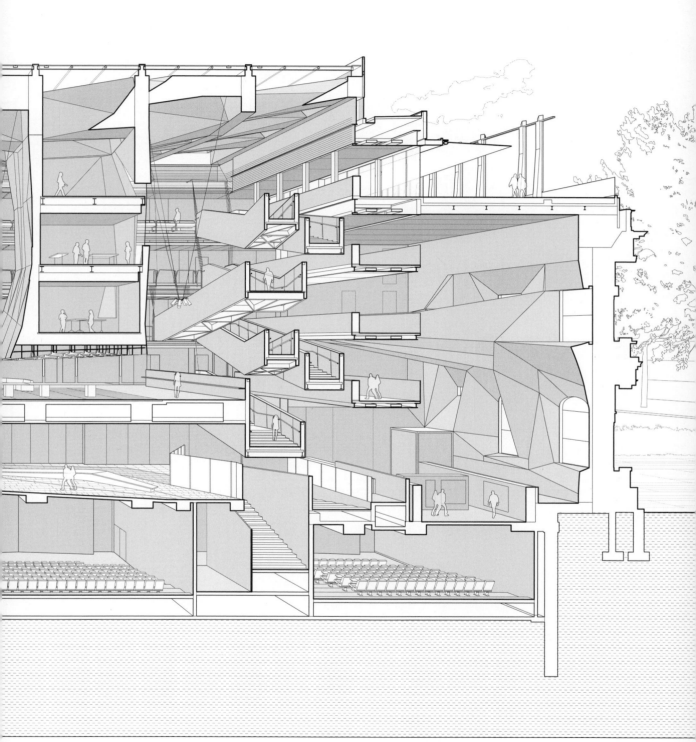

NADAAA / John Wardle Architects | 2014

an extension of the studios, as well as areas for impromptu collaboration. Two prominent architectural figures nest within the atrium space. The first is a series of robust ramps that provide the primary vertical circulation and expose their steel structure on their undersides. The second is a wood-clad volume containing studio space for visiting critics. This sculptural volume extends the faceted geometries of the coffered, light-diffusing ceiling from which it hangs. The building combines inclined, nested, shaped, stacked, and holed sections to produce a vibrant and instructive learning environment.

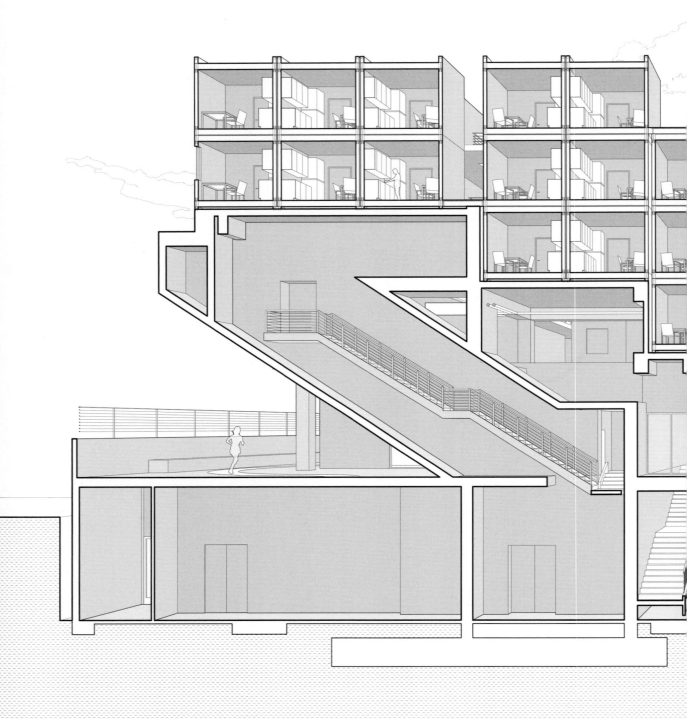

Star Apartments | Los Angeles, California, USA

This mixed-use building's alignment of program, structure, and section is legible in its massing. An existing single-story building was reworked to contain street-level retail spaces and a common entry to 102 apartments located on four new floors above, which are occupied by formerly homeless

individuals. These units were prefabricated in wood and stacked atop a terraced concrete platform, which is held above the existing building on concrete columns. The space between the new platform and the preexisting roof is shaped to provide space for a variety of outdoor communal programs,

Michael Maltzan Architecture | 2015

including a basketball court, gardens, and an exercise walkway loop. Three inclined volumes containing egress stairs are expressed externally as oblique figures appearing to dramatically hoist the apartments in the air. The modular apartments are stacked to allow for staggered exterior terraces and walkways. The building combines stacked, shaped, sheared, and holed sections to produce a rich combination of exterior and interior spaces for low-cost urban housing and community living.

Museum of Image and Sound | Rio de Janeiro, Brazil

Located along Rio de Janeiro's Copacabana Beach, this museum interlaces linked floors for exhibition and display with floors for retail and restaurants through an atrium defined by the vertical shear of those levels. In the rectangular plan, social and exhibition programs are located between

two linear bars of circulation, one interior and one exterior. A performance hall is positioned below grade, and an open-air cinema inhabits the roof. On the facade continuous exterior paths and elongated stairs extend the historic Roberto Burle Marx–designed street promenade up the side of the

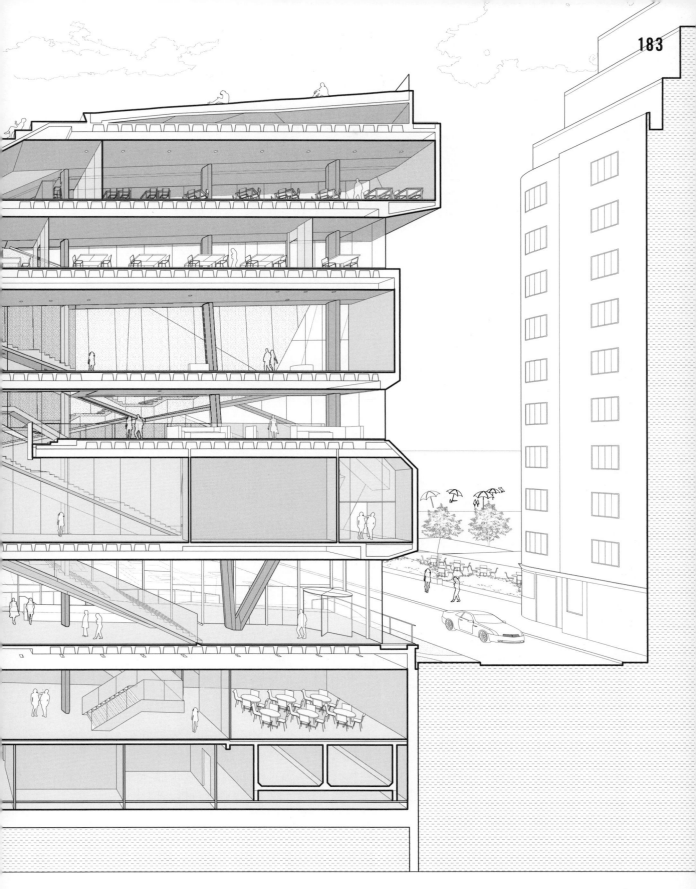

Diller Scofidio + Renfro | 2016

building, transgressing divisions between interior and exterior and allowing direct access to programs above the ground level. The figures of this vertical circulation provide the building's image. Along this vertical sequence a portion of the facade's skin is composed of custom open masonry block, choreographing views out of the museum and allowing light into the museum. Through an intricate combination of incline, stack, vertical shear, and hole, this section amplifies the social and cultural vitality of Rio de Janeiro.

In the work of LTL Architects, we foreground the section not only as a representational technique, ripe with the ability to demonstrate structure, interior space, and form, but also as a key locus of design invention. If the plan still absorbs much architectural interest, serving as a means to control function, organization, and movement, we argue that the section is the critical means for engaging social, environmental, and material

LTL IN SECTION

questions. Designing and thinking through section establishes a relationship among architectural form, interior space, and site, where the consequences of scale are tangible and visceral. As a cut into that which cannot be seen, the section embodies and reveals territories for architectural experimentation and exploration.

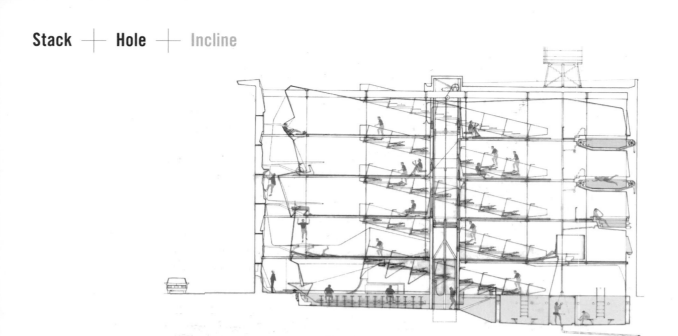

Sport Bars | New York, New York | 1997

This project collapses the distinctions among machines, bodies, and building in an urban health club and sports bar by linking discrete activities in section. Individual exercise machines are sutured into corresponding architectonic systems: the rock-climbing wall is the facade; weather membrane doubles as resistance membrane; elevator counterweights align with weight machines; plumbing lines couple swimming and bathing. By organizing these systems around three vertical shafts or holes that extend into the sports bar below, we offered sedentary patrons views of both televised sporting events and the activities in the gym above.

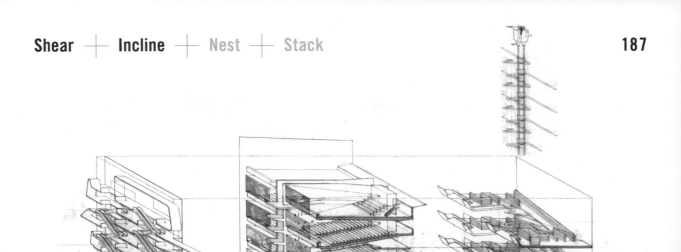

Video Filmplex | New York, New York | 1997

In this speculative project that examines the culture of filmgoing, we high-lighted sectional operations in nesting a series of shaped spaces, organized on inclines to enable unusual adjacencies between disparate programs. A video store occupies the interstitial space formed by the sloping of the theater floors. Restrooms are sandwiched between two stacks of theaters, allowing films to be watched even during bathroom breaks. The two stacks are sheared vertically, allowing us to design the facade as a continuous public space, linking the two sides of the Video Filmplex into one complex.

Stack ─┼─ Nest ─┼─ Hole

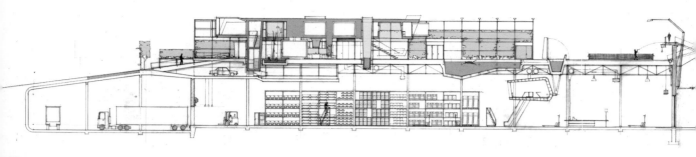

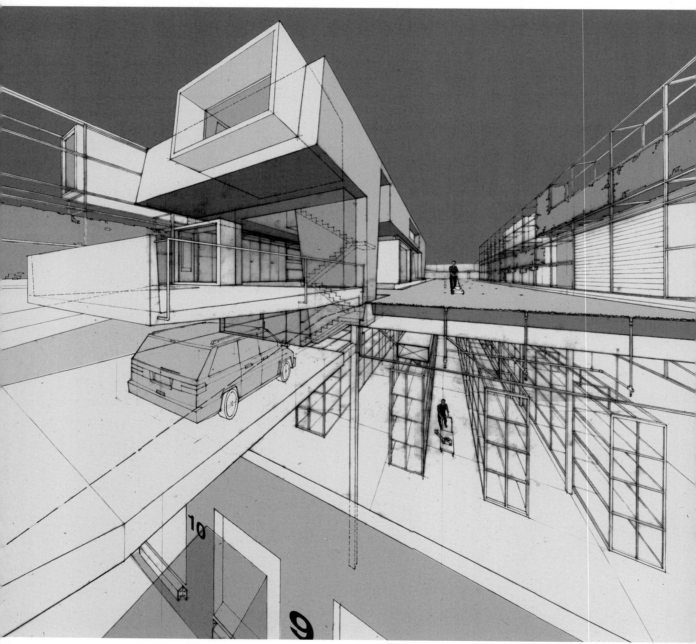

New Suburbanism │ Prototypical American Suburb │ 2000

This proposal embraces yet reconfigures the suburban desires for mini-mansions and big-box stores. We developed new sectional matings to accommodate the pursuit of the American dream while mitigating horizontal sprawl. Dwellings are stacked atop big-box stores' roofs, now turned into suburban fields. Both systems share structural and mechanical infrastructures, using section for new efficiencies. The residential neighborhood above maintains its autonomy from the commercial and parking zone below, despite their proximity. Physical and visual access is possible only by commuting around the block on inclined roads.

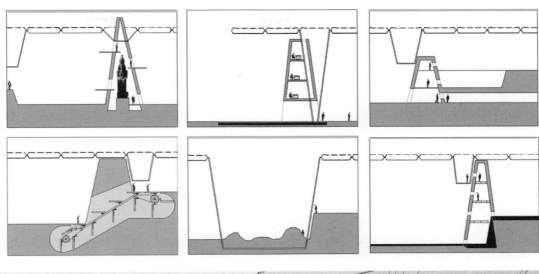

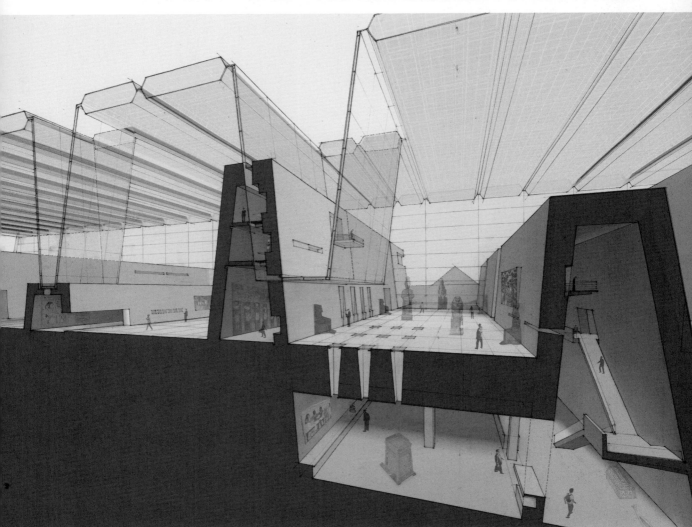

Great Egyptian Museum | Giza, Egypt | 2002

For this massive museum of 4.3 million sq ft, designed to house and exemplify the grand history of Egyptian art and culture, we used section to weave together ground and sky. A canopy of solar collectors and glass floats above a striated landscape of inhabitable pylons. Inverted glass-clad wedges drop from the sky, while battered stone pylons rise up from the desert plain. The varied sectional exchanges of these two figures provide an extensive repertoire of exhibition and display opportunities that integrate building, object, and landscape.

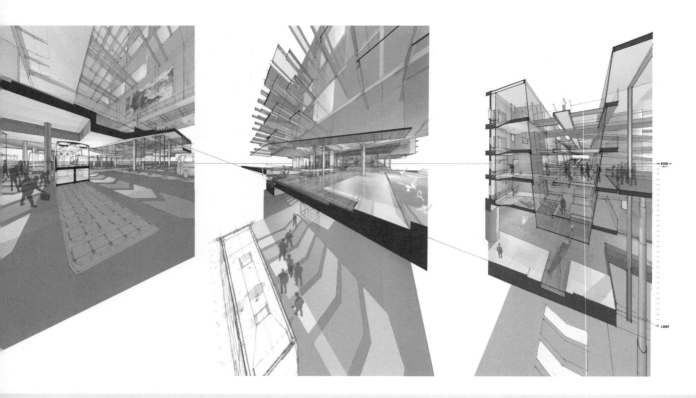

Tourbus Hotel │ Between Munich and Venice │ 2002

Located on the highway between two destination cities for tourists, this hotel exhibits a range of hybrid section types, intensifying the idiosyncratic organizational and social qualities of the European bus tour. Five stacked bars of rooms, sheared horizontally for access to sun and visually activated by holes along the corridor, are positioned above an open lobby that is part leisure landscape and part cruise ship deck. We organized programmatic adjacencies of the lobby though vertical shear and inclined sections. Ramps extend the lobby up through the rooms above, while oversized elevators link bus parking to the stack of programs.

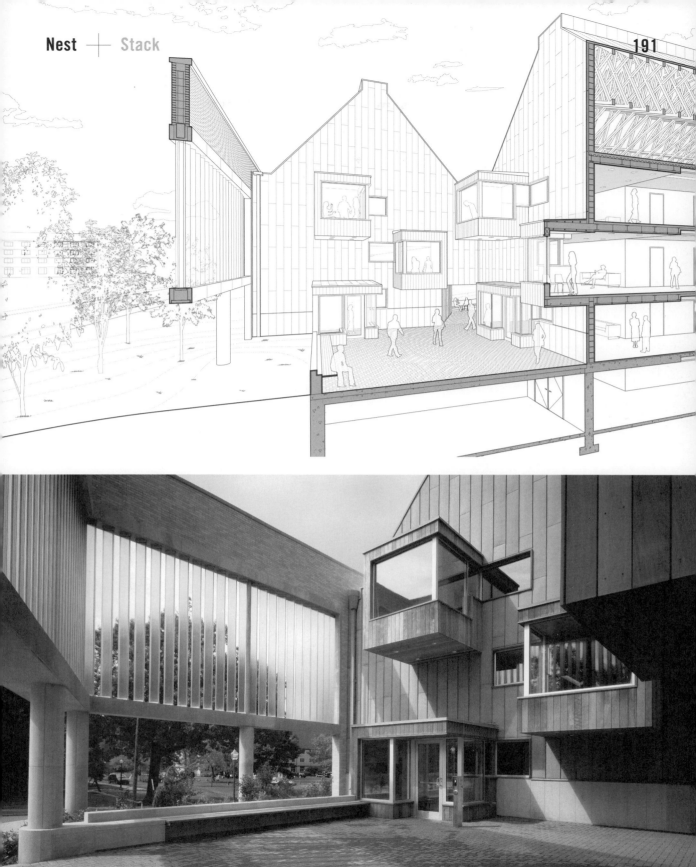

Bornhuetter Hall | Wooster, Ohio | 2004

For reasons of efficiency, security, acoustic control, and organizational hierarchy, residence halls are typically developed as stacked sections of discrete floors of rooms. To enhance social and visual exchanges within these constraints, we designed an exterior entry courtyard, contained within the building's skin, as the heart of the project. Cantilevered study rooms are nested within this volume, embedding private study within the collective setting. The daily activity of coming and going from the residence hall becomes a theatrical public event.

Incline ╋ Hole ╋ Shear ╋ Stack ╋ Nest

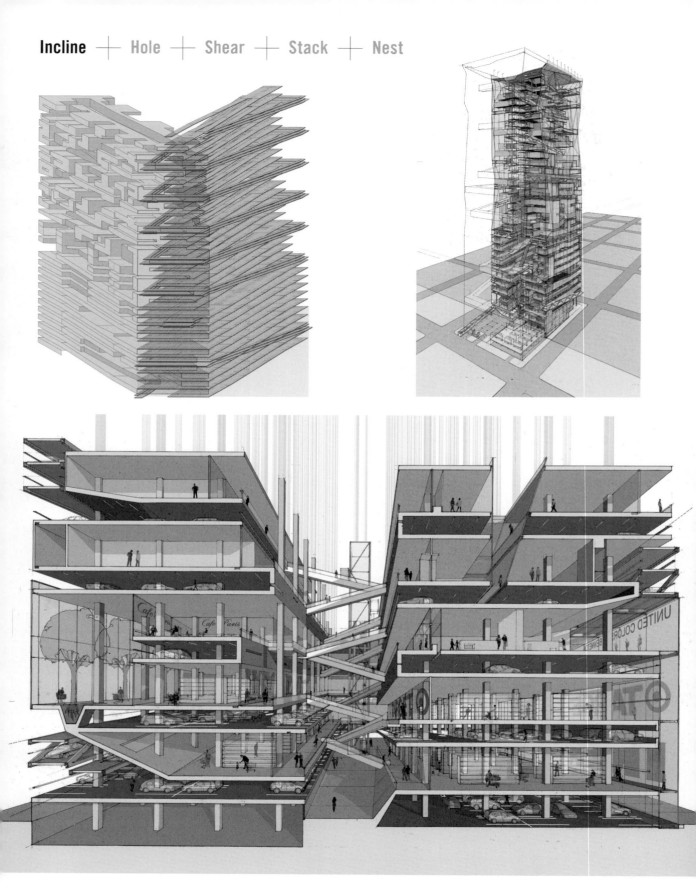

Park Tower | New York, New York | 2004

For this speculative tower, we exploited the properties of an inclined section to produce a drive-up skyscraper for zero-emissions vehicles, linking the stacked floor plates of the typical high-rise through a continuous spiral. Beginning with the logics of the switchback parking ramp, we intertwined a multilevel garage and a sandwich of inhabitable space, combining ubiquity of vehicular access with the pleasures of high-rise urban living. As the tower rises, this double-helix configuration mutates to accommodate a variety of sectional conditions, including a multistory atrium and voids offering light and views.

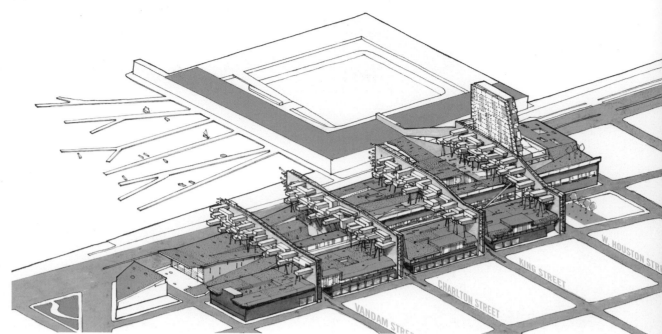

The Grid and the Superblock | New York, New York | 2007

Faced with the interruption of the pattern of the Manhattan grid by two early twentieth-century superblocks in downtown New York City, we asked how the very idiosyncrasies of these anomalous structures could sponsor a new urbanism animated in section. By extending the east-west street grid over these monoliths as a series of elevated housing bridges, we activated the massive rooftops as a raised urban ground, newly perforated by light courts and linked by inclined surfaces. While most of New York City remains spatially stratified, this proposal attempts to foster a fully multilevel urbanism.

Shape ─┼─ Nest ─┼─ Hole

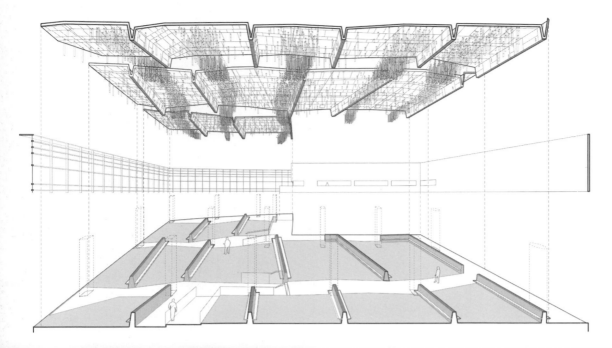

The Buffet at the MGM Grand | Las Vegas, Nevada | 2009

In designing this six-hundred-seat, all-you-can-eat dining facility we operated primarily through section to animate the dining experience within a standard extruded casino floor plate. We shaped the inserted floor and ceiling to define smaller areas within the overall space. The high backs of the banquette seats break up the large horizontal plan, while matching folds in the undulating ceiling reinforce the spatial definition of a series of nested volumes. A gap between these two folded surfaces creates a consistent horizontal cut across the dining area, preserving views of the serving stations and outside pool.

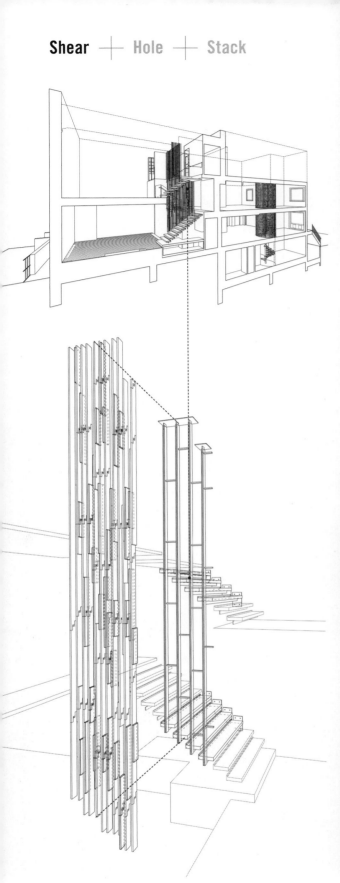

Spliced Townhouse | New York, New York | 2010

For this renovation of an existing prewar town house, we integrated six distinct floor levels in formerly separate apartments to create a spatially unified dwelling. Rather than attempting to erase these misalignments, we exposed and intensified the effects of this vertical shear while providing continuous access through a new steel and oak staircase. Partly cantilevered and partly suspended, the stair occupies the joint between the disparate floor plates, stitching together the various levels of the building while promoting visual interaction between spaces offset in section.

Hole ┼ Stack

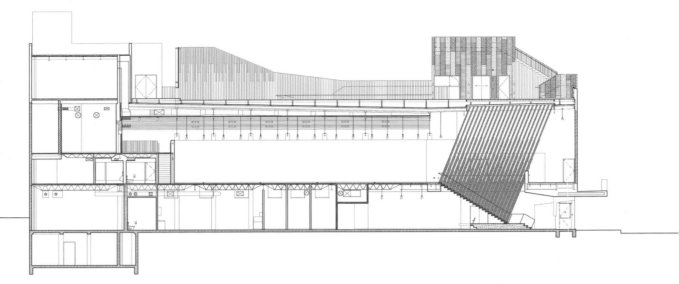

Arthouse | Austin, Texas | 2010

To activate the existing building's stacked section and entice visitors to move from this contemporary art center's lobby to its main second-floor gallery, we suspended a staircase from the roof through the full height of the building through holes cut in the floors. The vertical extensions of the twenty-one stair treads are inclined in two axes, with the slope derived from the geometry of the stair nosing. The logic of a minor detail informs the overall form in section. Due to these slopes, the stair's width expands as one ascends from the street level opening up to the large second-floor gallery.

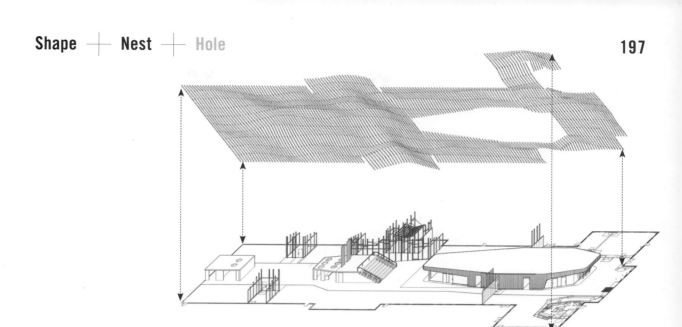

CUC Administrative Campus Center │ Claremont, California │ 2011

The conversion of an existing maintenance building into an open-office admin-istrative center was limited by its single-story extruded section. Nevertheless, we capitalized on the relatively high ceiling and the expansive column-free space to nest an array of individual meeting spaces and collective bleacher seating. We inserted a shaped ceiling of custom linear baffles throughout the building to unify the whole space. The cloudlike topography of baffles is adjusted to define social spaces and occlude views of mechanical systems, while still permitting natural light from skylights to pass.

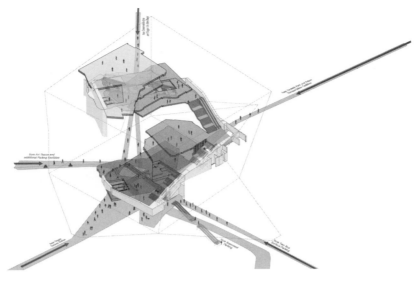

New Taipei City Museum of Art | New Taipei City, Taiwan | 2011

In this competition proposal for a museum of art, we organized the program as a single prismatic volume accessed from below via a continuous lobby. Combining aspects of both atrium and grand staircase, the lobby spirals up through the eight stacked floors of the building, shifting in response to external forces of view and light, as well as internal programmatic obligations. While the lobby forms a legible figure in plan at any given level, it is constantly changing and complex in section, creating a dynamic public promenade with aspects of shaped, inclined, and hole sectional typologies.

Living and Learning Residence Hall 6 | Washington DC | 2012

We used the hole's sectional capacities to disrupt the homogeneity of the dormitory type to meet Gallaudet University's DeafSpace standards. By inserting a void into the design of the repetitive stacked slab of this residence hall for deaf students, we created a four-story atrium, linking the four floors.

A main circulating staircase provides physical continuity. Large gaps between the void of the atrium and the inserted staircase permit visual exchanges that are key to enhancing communication and quality of life for the deaf residents.

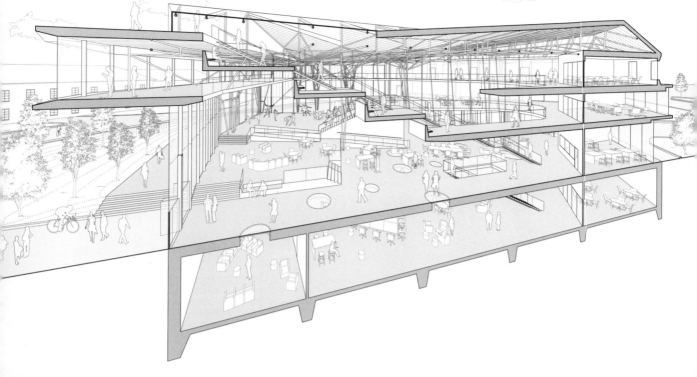

Liberal Arts College Campus Center │ Northeastern United States │ 2014

For this prototype for a campus center, we used incline and a unifying hole to intensify the relationship between collective space and traditional academic rooms. A central atrium organizes the required offices and classrooms at its perimeter. The atrium's floor is inclined and shaped to allow for programmatic specificity, diversity, and flexibility, engendering social exchanges along paths of travel. We designed the shaped ceiling and nested interior spaces for greater thermal performance, creating a gradient of temperature zones within the interior volume. The atrium extends the field of the campus up and through the building.

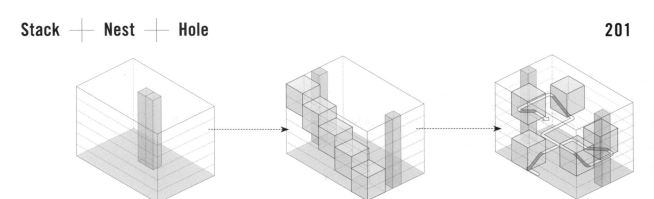

Office Building | New York, New York | 2015

In the competition design for the new offices of a philanthropic organization, we used a sequence of double-height volumes as sectional foils to the logic of efficient office plans. These five distinct spaces act as holes within the stacked floor plates, providing joints that form common spaces, libraries, and meeting rooms between levels. By integrating staircases into these spaces, we created the possibility of a continuous public promenade through the foundation, fostering communication and enabling unexpected encounters and exchanges among departments.

Sections by Height

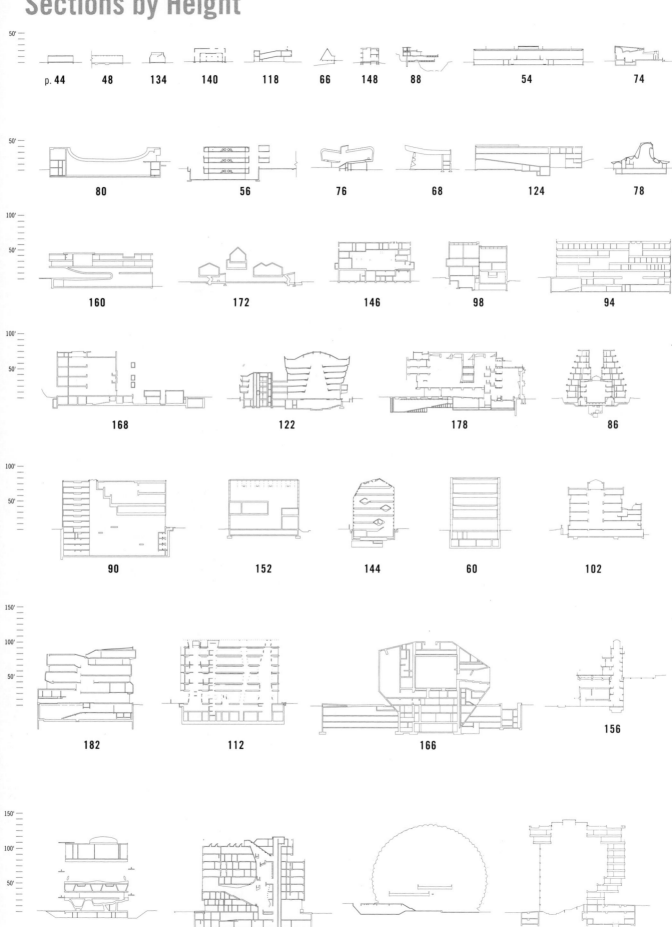

50'

p. 44   48   134   140   118   66   148   88   54   74

50'

80   56   76   68   124   78

100'
50'

160   172   146   98   94

100'
50'

168   122   178   86

100'
50'

90   152   144   60   102

150'
100'
50'

182   112   166   156

150'
100'
50'

62   114   138   106

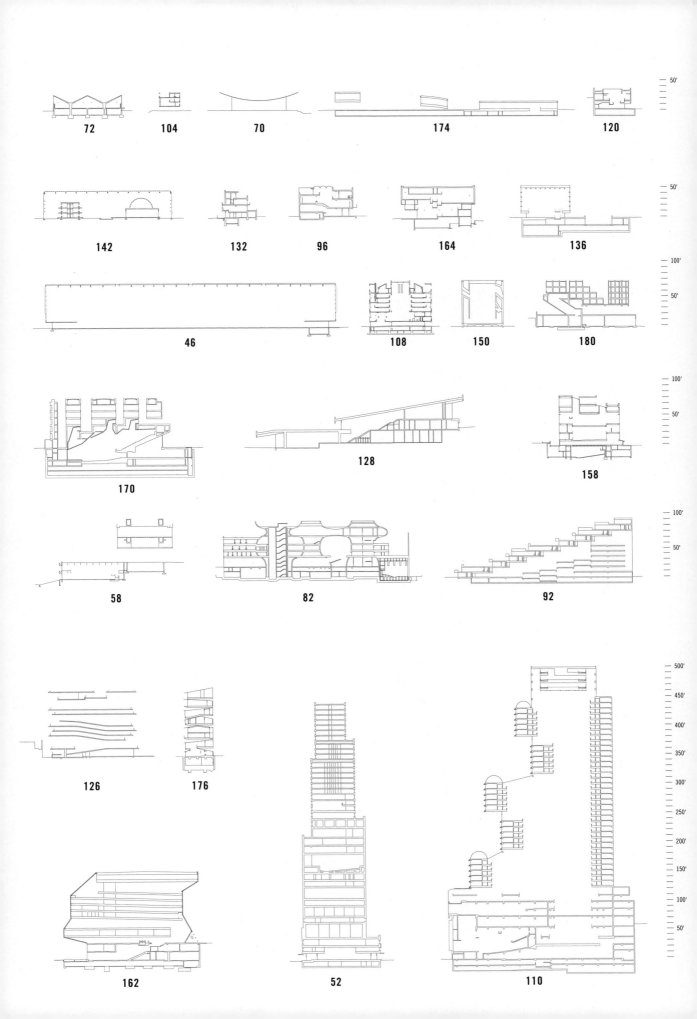

72 104 70 174 120

50'

142 132 96 164 136

50'

100'

50'

46 108 150 180

100'

50'

170 128 158

100'

50'

58 82 92

500'
450'
400'
350'
300'
250'
200'
150'
100'
50'

126 176

162 52 110

Index of Architects

Drawing Credits

Each of the sixty-three drawings in this book was produced through a multilayered process involving research, the careful examination of photographs and drawings, the production of digital models of the buildings, and the translation of those models into sectional perspectives composed of only lines. LTL Architects would like to thank the following people for their contributions to this book: Cyrus Peñarroyo and Alec Henry fulfilled crucial management responsibilities in the design and development of the book as a whole; Alec Henry also assisted in adjustments across all the drawings, as did Erica Alonzo, Kenneth Garnett, Jenny Hong, Christine Nasir and Corliss Ng. This book would not have been possible without the dedicated and precise efforts of many talented individuals. Below we recognize the people who worked on the drawings found on the listed page numbers. Although it was not uncommon for a number of people to be involved in each drawing over the course of its development, an asterisk denotes the completion of substantial aspects of the drawing's development.

Erica Alonzo
46*

Laura Britton
44 80* 82* 150*

Nerea Castell Sagües
54 76* 80 94* 106* 120* 122* 148 168

Debbie Chen
62* 70 78* 86 96* 110* 134 166* 168*

Erica Cho
104* 124* 180*

Kenneth Garnett
60 78 88 94 102 136 182

Kevin Hayes
76* 126* 136* 140*

Alec Henry
56 134* 162

Krithika Penedo
72* 74 78* 86 96* 126* 142*

Rennie Jones
56* 74 86 102 110* 140

Van Kluytenaar
94* 108* 128* 158* 178*

Anna Knoell
86 102 108 124 134 146 150

Zhongtian Lin
44 48 62* 66 70* 74 82* 92* 108*
110* 112* 128 136* 140 144 156*
160* 162 164 172* 180*

Lindsey May
54* 62 74 90 92 96 102 110 112
120 152* 160*

Asher McGlothlin
136

Cyrus Peñarroyo
52* 60* 68* 72 74 90* 98 114 132*
138* 150 152* 170* 174* 176*

Anika Schwarzwald
56 68 72 88 118 120 126 132 140

Hannah Sellers
86 94

Abby Stone
66* 118* 146* 148* 152* 164*

Yen-Ju Tai
138

Regina Teng
48* 58* 60* 74* 104* 144* 172

Antonia Wai
98* 102* 114* 158* 162* 164 166*
176 178* 182*

Chao Lun Wang
88* 102*

Tamara Yurovsky
54* 56 162*

Weijia Zhang
128 146

The sixty-three drawings in this book are the work and interpretation of LTL Architects, executed within the offices of LTL Architects. Work for this publication has been partially supported by Princeton University School of Architecture and by Parsons School of Design at The New School. No unpaid intern labor was used in the production of this work.

Acknowledgments

This book is the result of many years of collaborative work that has relied on the generosity and support of institutions, firms, colleagues, friends, and families. We acknowledge the patience and multiple talents of the staff of LTL Architects, who have been essential to its development, participating in the early discussions and final critiques. Throughout this book's development, we have been encouraged and supported by peers who have generously given of their time and insights to inform the discourse on section. In particular we would like to thank Stan Allen, Stella Betts, Dana Cuff, David Leven, Arnold Lewis, Beth Irwin Lewis, Guy Nordenson, Nat Oppenheimer, Peter Pelsinski, Jonsara Ruth, Karen Stonely, Enrique Walker, Saundra Weddle, Robert Weddle, Sarah Whiting, and Ron Witte, whose keen observations at formative stages of this project have enriched and strengthened this publication. We offer our gratitude to colleagues who have given of their time and resources to ensure the accuracy and clarity of the drawings of their work, including Gerard Carty, Elizabeth Diller, Michael Maltzan, Michael Manfredi, Chris McVoy, Charles Renfro, Shoji Sadao, Ricardo Scofidio, Nader Tehrani, Marion Weiss, and Robert Wennett.

We are grateful to all the architects and engineers whose collective work has built the discourse of architecture from which the argument and sections for this publication are drawn. In the creation of the section-perspective drawings for the sixty-three projects that make up the main portion of this publication, we are grateful to the assistance and generosity of the following individuals and entities: the Alvar Aalto Museum; aceboXalonso Studio; the Avery Architectural and Fine Arts Library at Columbia University; Institute Lino Bo and P. M. Bardi; Bjarke Ingels Group; the Marcel Breuer Digital Archive, Syracuse University Libraries; R. Buckminster Fuller Collection at Stanford University Library; Cité de L'architecture et du Patrimoine; Diller Scofidio + Renfro; Studio Fuksas; Grafton Architects; Henning Larsen Architects; Architectuurstudio HH; Steven Holl Architects; Toyo Ito & Associates, Architects; Jourda Architectes Paris; Louis I. Kahn Collection at the Architectural Archives of the University of Pennsylvania; Kengo Kuma and Associates; Fondation Le Corbusier; Michael Maltzan Architecture; Morphosis; the Charles Moore Foundation; the Ludwig Mies van der Rohe Archive at the Museum of Modern Art; MVRDV; NADAA; Neutelings Riedijk Architects; OMA; Pezo Von Ellrichshausen; John Portman & Associates; Kevin Roche John Dinkeloo and Associates Records in the Manuscripts & Archives of the Yale University Library; Robert A. M. Stern; Paul Marvin Rudolph Archive at the Library of Congress; Rudolph M. Schindler Archive at the Architecture & Design Collection in the University Art Museum at the University of California, Santa Barbara; Mack Scogin Merrill Elam Architects; Weiss/Manfredi; and the Frank Lloyd Wright Foundation Archives at the Avery Architectural and Fine Arts Library at Columbia University.

We thank Princeton Architectural Press for its long-standing support and encouragement for the completion of this book. Special thanks goes to editors Megan Carey, who offered valuable insight and guidance in the early stages of the project, and Sara Stemen, for her precise feedback and patience in bringing the publication to fruition. Our gratitude extends as well to Kevin Lippert for his continued commitment to the discourse of architecture through the cultivation of books.

Finally, we offer heartfelt gratitude to our families for encouraging and enabling the completion of this work—Daina Tsurumaki, Toshi Tsurumaki, Chris Tsurumaki, Beth Irwin Lewis, Arnold Lewis, and Martha Lewis.

Image Credits

Published by Princeton Architectural Press
A division of Chronicle Books LLC
70 West 36th Street, New York, New York 10018
papress.com

© 2016 Princeton Architectural Press
All rights reserved. Printed and bound in China.
24 23 22   9 8 7

Editor: Sara Stemen   Design: Lewis.Tsurumaki.Lewis

Special thanks to: Janet Behning, Nicola Brower, Abby Bussel, Erin Cain, Tom Cho, Barbara Darko, Benjamin English, Jenny Florence, Jan Cigliano Hartman, Lia Hunt, Mia Johnson, Valerie Kamen, Simone Kaplan-Senchak, Stephanie Leke, Diane Levinson, Jennifer Lippert, Sara McKay, Jaime Nelson Noven, Rob Shaeffer, Paul Wagner, Joseph Weston, and Janet Wong of Princeton Architectural Press —Kevin C. Lippert, publisher

Library of Congress Cataloging-in-Publication Data:
Names: Lewis, Paul, 1966– author. | Tsurumaki, Marc, 1965– author. | Lewis, David J., 1966– author.
Title: Manual of Section / Paul Lewis, Marc Tsurumaki, David J. Lewis.
Description: First edition. | New York : Princeton Architectural Press, 2016 | Includes index.
Identifiers: LCCN 2015047210 | ISBN 9781616892555 (alk. paper)
Subjects: LCSH: Architectural sections. | Architecture, Modern—20th century—Designs and plans. | Architecture, Modern—21st century—Designs and plans.
Classification: LCC NA2775 .L49 2016 | DDC 724/.6—dc23
LC record available at http://lccn.loc.gov/2015047210

This book
is dedicated to:

Kim Yao
Sarabeth Lewis Yao
Maximo Lewis Yao
—Paul Lewis

Carmen Lenzi
Kai Luca Tsurumaki
Lucia Alise Tsurumaki
—Marc Tsurumaki

Quinn Arnold Lewis
Jonsara Ruth
—David J. Lewis